DEEP
COMMITMENTS

DEEP COMMITMENTS

THE PAST, PRESENT, AND FUTURE OF RELIGIOUS LIBERTY

EDITED BY TREVOR BURRUS AND DAVID MCDONALD

CATO INSTITUTE
WASHINGTON, D.C.

ebook ISBN: 978-1-944424-82-4
Print ISBN: 978-1-9444-81-7

Library of Congress Cataloging-in-Publication Data available.

Cover design: Jon Meyers.

Printed in the United States of America.

CATO INSTITUTE
1000 Massachusetts Avenue, N.W.
Washington, D.C. 20001
www.cato.org

To the Jehovah's Witnesses, the Arians, the Amish, the Protestants, the Catholics, and all other religious groups who peacefully fought for their religious freedoms and, in the process, fought for all our freedoms.

To all the participants in the conference and the contributors to this volume, without whom these pages would be empty.

Contents

SECTION II: RELIGION AND EDUCATION: THE CONSTANT BATTLEGROUND

SECTION III: PUBLIC ACCOMMODATION: WHAT ARE THE LIMITS?

Acknowledgments

Thank you to Devin Watkins, Frank Garrison, and Thomas Berry for help with transcribing the speeches. Special thanks to David McDonald not only for helping with transcriptions, but also for editing the question-and-answer sessions and helping compile the book in its final form.

Thank you to Neal McCluskey, Roger Pilon, and Ilya Shapiro for helping organize the original event, and thank you to Roger for bringing the book to publication.

Thank you to John Samples, David Lampo, and the entire Cato publications team.

Last, but certainly not least, we'd like to thank the Bradley Foundation, whose generous contribution made the conference possible.

Preface

In June 2016, the Cato Institute convened a daylong conference, "Protecting Religious Liberty." Because issues surrounding religious liberty affect a variety of public policy areas, the conference brought together scholars from Cato's Center for Constitutional Studies, its Center for Educational Freedom, and a number of distinguished outside scholars. Consisting of three panels and two keynote speakers, the conference addressed the history and philosophy of religious freedom, religious freedom and education, and current controversies over religious freedom and public accommodations. Given the quality of the presentations, we decided to adapt the talks into the book you now have before you, to which introductory and concluding essays have been added.

The introduction by editor Trevor Burrus, research fellow in Cato's Center for Constitutional Studies, gives an overview of the history of religious toleration and its importance to the development of Enlightenment liberalism. From there the book moves to the keynote address by Professor Douglas Laycock of the University of Virginia School of Law. Focusing on the battles over the Religious Freedom Restoration Act (RFRA), Professor Laycock looks at how religious liberty fares in the current culture wars.

Section I explores various aspects of the history and philosophy of religious liberty. John M. Barry, author of a recent book on Roger Williams, discusses Williams's fascinating life and his underappreciated contributions to the American tradition of religious liberty. Next is Robert P. George, the McCormick Professor of Jurisprudence at Princeton University and director of the James Madison Program in American Ideals and Institutions, who discusses the role religious liberty plays in promoting human well-being. To round out the section, Doug Bandow, senior fellow at the Cato Institute, discusses the relationship between the growth of government and an increasing number of conflicts with religious liberty.

The second section focuses on the seemingly endless conflicts over the role of religion in public education. Charles L. Glenn, a professor of educational leadership who has spent more than 40 years working to improve educational equity and freedom, argues that only structural pluralism, encouraging a wide variety of schools of different religious and political persuasions for parents to choose from, can reconcile the public provision of education with principles of religious liberty. Next, Jonathan Zimmerman, professor of education and history and director of the History of Education Program at New York University's Steinhardt School of Culture, Education, and Human Development, discusses the need for schools to prepare students to tackle the tough and contentious issues surrounding the role of religion in public life with civility and open minds. Charles C. Haynes, vice president of the Newseum Institute and executive director of the Religious Freedom Center, then discusses the importance, in a country as religiously diverse as ours, of the First Amendment in providing a shared civic framework within which we can teach students of all faiths how to work toward understanding and common ground. Finally, Neal McCluskey, director of Cato's Center for Educational Freedom, argues that public schooling, in a pluralistic society, inevitably leads to religious conflict and discrimination. Therefore, unless we want to continue fighting over our deeply held values, we should consider replacing our standard public education model with a voucher or tax credit system or, at the very least, provide more avenues for parents to move their children outside the traditional public school and into schools that comport with their values.

The book's final section discusses public accommodation laws and the tension between religious liberty principles, on the one hand, and equal protection anti-discrimination principles, on the other. Roger Pilon, vice president for legal affairs at the Cato Institute and founding director of Cato's Center for Constitutional Studies, explores the ways in which an expanding federal government, unmoored from the Constitution's limitations, has necessarily constricted the realm in which people are free to publicly exercise their religious beliefs. Next, Mark L. Rienzi, associate professor at The Catholic University of America, Columbus School of Law, discusses how public accommodations laws have been used to enforce conformity and wipe out politically disfavored opinions. Finally, Louise Melling, deputy legal director at the American Civil Liberties Union and the director of its Center for Liberty, offers a contrary view, arguing that religious exemptions to public accommodations laws cause very real harm to those who are denied service and that religious liberty does not entail the right to discriminate.

Concluding the main body of the book is an essay by the Honorable William H. Pryor of the U.S. Court of Appeals for the Eleventh Circuit, who gave the closing address of the conference. Judge Pryor discusses how our legal tradition of protecting religious liberty has respected the right of religious people to be left alone. He also explores the important question of how faith should or should not inform a religious judge's work. Following Judge Pryor's remarks, the book concludes with an essay by Ilya Shapiro, senior fellow in constitutional studies at the Cato Institute and editor-in-chief of the *Cato Supreme Court Review*, on how modern battles over religion in the public square are a microcosm of the constant tension between civil society and an overweening regulatory state.

We hope you enjoy *Deep Commitments: The Past, Present, and Future of Religious Liberty.*

1. Introduction: The Cleansing Fire of Religious Liberty

Trevor Burrus

On December 24, 361 CE, an angry mob broke into a prison in Alexandria, Egypt. The mob was made up of both pagans and Christians, two factions that usually were fighting each other rather than rioting together. Over the previous decade, riots had become disturbingly common in Alexandria, which was one of the most important cities for both Christianity and paganism. The riots were often rooted in religious disagreement, and this one was no different.[1]

The object of the mob's passion was George of Cappadocia, the bishop of Alexandria and an important figure in the Egyptian Christian community. But "important" does not always mean well liked, and although George was the titular head of the Christian church in the area, approximately half of the local Christians despised him. George of Cappadocia was an Arian, which to many Christians was an unforgivable heresy.

Arianism was one of the most significant and common "heresies" in the history of Christianity. Although the word is rarely used now, for most of Christian history the charge of "Arianism" was both extremely common and extremely dangerous. Arians were Christians, just like those who lit the matches to burn them at the stake. Of course, there were many who would deny them the name "Christian"—thus the riots and violence—but, on the most basic level, Arians worshiped and devoted their lives to the teachings of Jesus Christ. Yet unlike "mainstream"

1

Christianity—an odd phrase because Arians sometimes outnumbered non-Arians—they believed that Jesus was "merely" the Son of God rather than God himself, thus denying the Trinity. And that was regarded as no minor quibble by either side.

Alexandria was in many ways the focal point of the battle between Arians and non-Arians. Only a few years before the mob arrived at the prison, the bishop of Alexandria had been Athanasius, one of the most important figures in early Christian history. Athanasius was an anti-Arian, and during his tenure as bishop, he had used beatings, intimidation, kidnappings, excommunications, and exile to eliminate or coerce into submission the dangerously heretical Arians. But Athanasius had been removed from his position by Constantius, the son of Constantine the Great and an Arian himself. In his place, Constantius put George of Cappadocia, telling the Alexandrians that the new bishop was "the most perfect of beings as a guide for your conduct, both in word and deed."[2]

George hardly fared better than Athanasius. Alexandria's Christians were fairly evenly divided between Arians and anti-Arians, so half the Christian population was sure to be upset by the choice of bishop. In addition, George engaged in a "carefully orchestrated anti-pagan campaign" that "marked a new stage in the official coercion of religious dissent in Alexandria."[3] After being attacked in the church of St. Dionysius in August of 358, George decided to leave the city.[4] During his three-year sojourn, George participated in church councils to try to resolve the "Arian controversy." Those councils declared Arian beliefs orthodox (but their determinations were not accepted by all, e.g., Athanasius), so George decided to return to Alexandria in November of 361. Unfortunately and unbeknownst to him, only three weeks before he arrived back in Alexandria, Constantius, his imperial patron and protector, died. Lacking Constantius's backing, George of Cappadocia was imprisoned, and a short time later George heard the shouts of the mob as they came to get rid of him once and for all.

The mob emerged from the prison with three shackled prisoners in tow—George and two high government officials, Draconitis and Diodorus, both of whom had been disrespectful to some of the city's pagan religions.[5] All three were beaten to death in the prison square, and their bodies were paraded around the city. The mob later burned the bodies to ensure that no saint's relics could be collected from the remains.[6]

***

The unfortunate death of George of Cappadocia is not particularly unique in the history of Christianity. In the words of one scholar, "Of all the great world religions past and present, Christianity has been by far the most intolerant."[7] Although some may contest the characterization of Christianity as "by far the most intolerant," it is at least vexing that a religion based on the teachings of a heretical outcast who believed in mutual love and nonviolence could so easily be converted into a religion of bishops being murdered in the streets, auto-da-fés, and burnings at the stake.

Yet it must be equally vexing to consider how Christianity, and the Western world more broadly, became the center of religious toleration—meaning toleration based not just on pragmatic or political reasons, but also on respect for individual autonomy. For most liberals—in the classical sense—the idea of freedom of religion or, as it was often called, liberty of conscience, is a foundational tenet of Enlightenment thought. And for some, such as John Stuart Mill, liberty of conscience was the "first of all the articles of the liberal creed."[8]

In this essay, I will give one interpretation of how the ideas of religious toleration evolved in the West, and how, eventually, liberty of conscience came to be regarded as one of the cornerstones of the Western liberal political tradition. Like many fundamental elements of our post-Enlightenment world—freedom of speech and private property, for example—liberty of conscience is easily taken for granted. Many modern, post-Enlightenment citizens have difficulties formulating arguments against the liberty of conscience because they regard it as obvious that governments have no legitimate power over the beliefs of their citizens. To argue otherwise is to promote despotism and totalitarianism.

But the general inability to formulate arguments against liberty of conscience means that the arguments *for* liberty of conscience have gone largely untested, if not grown wholly atrophied due to desuetude. While widespread belief in the liberty of conscience is one of the most important developments in modern political history—after all, its popularity offers one of the best protections against would-be despots—the fact that it is so widespread and so unquestionably accepted means that, for many, the provenance of this tenet of liberalism has been forgotten. In a sense, it's like the religious doctrines of old: widely believed and little understood.

Moreover, by exploring the history of religious toleration and the liberty of conscience, we can more broadly explore the history of liberalism in general. After all, the Western world was once a disturbingly illiberal place. Notions of individual rights were subsumed to a theory of overarching power that mixed together theories of religious authority with inchoate views of the "nation." Medieval political debates—insofar as the concept of "political" had meaning—focused on delineating the *sacerdotium* from the *regnum*—that is, the areas controlled by priestly, spiritual power versus the areas controlled by secular, monarchical power. But, in the words of intellectual historian George H. Smith, "it is misleading to view these realms as analogous to church and state in the modern sense, for *sacerdotium* and *regnum* were conceived as aspects of the same universal society—the *Ecclesia*, a single community composed of all Christians."[9]

All power in this system flowed from God. The kings of the *regnum* claimed authority over their subjects (they certainly were not citizens in any modern sense of the word) as either given by God to them or given by God to the people who then passed it on to the ruler. Others asserted that all of that godly power must flow through the pope, God's chosen representative on earth, and therefore the pope held proper authority over all secular authorities. One thing was certain: whichever theory was preferred, there was very little room to assert a "right" to individual action or belief.

Yet somehow that deeply illiberal world was transformed into a political order in which liberal assertions of individual rights are, at least ostensibly, the cornerstone of modern political discourse. It is worth exploring that evolution further.

***

In Geneva, almost 1,200 years after George of Cappadocia met his unfortunate fate, Michael Servetus, another Arian, was bound to a stake and burned alive. Servetus was certainly not the last Arian to be tortured and punished for his views, but he became one of the most famous.

Michael Servetus was born in 1511 in a small town in northeast Spain. A gifted child, he learned Latin and Greek from Dominican Friars, studied law, and eventually became a doctor. Like many Renaissance and Reformation intellectuals, he was a polymath, writing or teaching in areas such as mathematics, astronomy, geography, and pharmacology. In 1531, he definitively announced his Arian views when he published *De Trinitatis Erroribus* (*On the Errors of the Trinity*), followed by *Dialogorum de Trinitate* (*Dialogues on the Trinity*) the next year. Servetus knew he had put himself in danger, and he changed his name to Michel de Villeneuve while he continued to study and write about medicine.[10]

In 1553, Servetus published *Christianismi Restitutio* (*The Restoration of Christianity*). Like many Renaissance and medieval works, *Christianismi Restitutio* is a massive tome that touches on many subjects. At one point, Servetus theorizes on the heart's role in pulmonary circulation—fully 75 years before William Harvey would receive credit for this discovery.[11] Despite its commentary on medicine and other subjects, the book is fundamentally a work of theology, and in it Servetus returned to attacking the Trinity as well as criticizing the ideas of predestination and infant baptism.

These arguments riled John Calvin, the founder of Calvinism and one of the central figures of the Reformation, who began a correspondence with Servetus and eventually developed a near-vendetta against him.

Christianismi Restitutio got Servetus into trouble in Vienne, France, where a follower of Calvin denounced him as a heretic. He was imprisoned but escaped. He then was convicted in absentia of "heresy, sedition, rebellion, and evasion of prison."[12] The tribunal ordered that his possessions be confiscated and, if caught, that he be burned at the stake.[13]

Servetus planned to flee to a group of friendly dissidents in Naples, Italy. En route, in a move that has "puzzled scholars for centuries," he stopped in Geneva, which was essentially a theocracy run by Calvin.[14] His intent was to stay only one day, but unfortunately he arrived the day before the Sabbath, when church attendance was mandatory. In a move even more inexplicable than stopping in Geneva, Servetus chose to attend services at the Madeleine, where Calvin himself would be preaching. He was recognized and captured.

Calvin could hardly believe his good luck. In short order, Servetus was put on trial. At one point during the proceedings, in a scene resembling the courtroom debates of *Inherit the Wind*, Calvin and Servetus went toe-to-toe on the differences between the divine substance and material things. But whether or not he prevailed in a debate with Calvin, even in open court, Servetus's conviction was essentially foreordained: he was sentenced to die.

They wrapped an iron chain around his body and lashed his neck to the stake with rope. On his head, they placed a crown of straw, leaves, and sulfur; and a copy of *Christianismi Restitutio* was tied to his arm. Because he was burned with fresh, green wood at his feet, it took 30 minutes for him to die. True to his beliefs to the last, witnesses reported hearing him scream "Oh Jesus, Son of the Eternal God, have pity on me!" If he had given up his Arian beliefs, he would have said, "Oh Jesus, Eternal Son of God."[15]

Calvin ordered that all copies of *Christianismi Restitutio* in Geneva be destroyed, and other copies were destroyed throughout Europe. Today, only three copies are known to exist, one of which seems to have been John Calvin's.

***

George of Cappadocia was killed by a mob and Servetus was killed by the state—or at least a theocratic tribunal wrapped up in the trappings of the state. The point is significant, because the early Christian church generally eschewed murdering dissidents. Shun, ostracize, and admonish them, certainly, and maybe occasionally subject them to corporal punishment, yes; but the early church generally treated heretics with a lighter touch than later generations did.

The early church, however, was subordinate to a secular power, the Roman Empire, and was often persecuted by it. Without state power, the church was a voluntary organization that lacked either the power or the ability to vigorously persecute those who disagreed or refused to join. Not until the Roman Empire accepted Christianity and then adopted it as a state religion did the persecution of heretics became a more official function. George of Cappadocia was murdered during a unique time in Christian history, a time when a diversity of "Christianities"—an overarching term meaning the numerous religions that focused their beliefs around Jesus Christ—fought over the meaning of "orthodoxy" and, in particular, what that would mean once the Roman Empire was embracing rather than persecuting Christians.[16] In 385, Maximus, coemperor of the western part of the empire, executed Priscillian, an advocate of a strict form of Christian asceticism that avoided churches and formality. It was the first recorded execution for heresy.[17]

In 407, the emperor Arcadius made heresy a public crime. In 510, Anastasius announced that Manicheans would receive the death penalty. And in 529, the emperor Justinian ordered all pagans and their families to receive baptism. State power and church power had begun to merge, and they would continue to merge, more or less, throughout the Middle Ages.[18]

By the medieval period, killing heretics had become church policy and, by extension, a state policy. At the Fourth Lateran Council in 1215, the church adopted the following canon:

> The secular authorities, whatever office they may hold, shall be admonished and induced and if necessary compelled [to] strive in good faith and to the best of their ability to exterminate in the territories subject to their jurisdiction all heretics pointed out by the Church.[19]

Aquinas put it even more bluntly: heretics "deserve not only to be separated from the Church by excommunication, but also to be severed from the world by death."[20]

It was a dangerous time for anyone to entertain thoughts that went against church doctrine, which is why Martin Luther's nailing of 95 theses to the door of the church in Wittenburg had significance beyond a mere religious, doctrinal dispute. Such independent thinking was a seed of a revolutionary idea: liberty of conscience. In many ways, liberty of conscience is the cornerstone of the Reformation. To deny the Catholic Church's sole and unimpeachable authority to interpret the Bible, to assert that individuals had both the ability and the duty to make up their own minds on scripture, was a radical assertion of liberty of conscience. Luther's famous words in response to the Diet of Worms (1521) said it all: "Here I stand; I can do no other."[21]

In a Europe that was being slowly upended by the Reformation, Michael Servetus's death and Calvin's revenge-based motivations sparked a prolonged controversy among intellectuals. In the words of Stefan Zweig, "it was immediately recognized that the burning of Servetus had brought the Reformation to and beyond a parting of the ways."[22] Zweig continues, "Throughout the centuries, among numberless atrocities, it has always been one, which might have seemed no worse than the others, that pricked apparently slumbering consciences."[23] Theodore Beza, one of Calvin's closest allies and essentially an inerrantist when it came to the ideas of his superior, wrote, "The ashes of the unhappy man were not yet cold when acrimonious discussion arose on the question whether heretics ought to be punished." In Geneva, Calvin had to call in police to stifle dissenters, including a woman imprisoned for declaring Servetus a martyr.[24] Even Edward Gibbon, writing more than 200 years later, said that he was "more deeply scandalized by the single execution of Servetus than at the hecatombs which have blazed in the Auto da Fés of Spain and Portugal."[25]

Why did Calvin do it? Did not Protestants, more than anyone at the time, stand for an individual's right to rethink and question dogma?

***

The most remarkable of Servetus's defenders was Sebastian Castellio. Castellio was born in 1515 in Dauphiné, France. A voracious learner who was highly regarded by his peers, he became a Protestant missionary in 1540 after seeing Protestant martyrs burned in Lyon.[26]

For a time, Castellio had Calvin's esteem, and he was even appointed as rector of the College of Geneva at Calvin's request. But Castellio's tendency to contradict Calvin, if not outright argue against him in public, soon rankled Calvin. When Castellio was unanimously appointed to the priesthood by the town authorities, Calvin strenuously objected. When asked to state his objections in public, Calvin cited two trifling theological differences—that Castellio regarded the Song of Solomon as a profane rather than sacred work and that Castellio described Jesus's descent to hell differently than Calvin did—as sufficient reason to withhold Castellio's appointment. Given the chance to adjust his views on these matters to secure the position, Castellio refused, citing his inability to go against his conscience.[27] At one public meeting, Castellio asked whether punishing those who hold different views made any sense given the fallibility of even the most exalted priest.

Calvin made sure that Castellio was charged with undermining "the prestige of the clergy," and he was suspended from his small preaching position.[28] Soon after, Castellio left Geneva.

When he heard about Servetus's fate at the hands of his old adversary, Castellio was understandably mortified. In a small tract, *Against Calvin's Book*, written shortly after Servetus's death, Castellio questioned Calvin (in dialogue form): "Since he opposed you in writings, why did you oppose [him] with iron and flame? Do you call this the defence of the pious magistrate? To kill a man is not to defend a doctrine, but to kill a man."[29]

But Calvin's crime against Servetus demanded a deeper discussion, so Castellio published a remarkable little book: *Concerning Heretics: Whether they are to be persecuted and how they are to be treated; a collection of the opinions of learned men, both ancient and modern; a most timely book in the view of the present turbulence and highly instructive to all and especially to princes and magistrates to show them their duty in a matter so controversial and dangerous*, which is usually shortened to *Concerning Heretics*. Given what had happened to Servetus, Castellio was smart enough to publish the book under a pseudonym, "Martinus Bellius," and to change the city of publication printed on the title page from Basel (where the book was actually published) to Magdeburg.

As the book's lengthy title describes, it is mostly a collection of opinions of "learned men" on the issue of toleration. Included are selections from Martin Luther, Erasmus, the early church father John Chrysostom, and even John Calvin himself. Surely with a smile on his lips, Castellio threw Calvin's words back at him. Calvin wrote in the first edition of his *Institutes of the Christian Religion*:

> Although ecclesiastical discipline does not permit familiarity and intimacy with the excommunicate, nevertheless we should try by every means, whether by exhortation and teaching, clemency and mildness, or by our prayers to God, to bring them to a better mind that they may return to the society and unity of the Church.[30]

Castellio dedicated *Concerning Heretics* to Christoph, Duke of Württemberg, and used the dedication to express his own views on religious tolerance, all the while asking the duke rhetorical questions such as "would you condemn such a citizen? I do not think so."[31]

Castellio wonders why heretics are singled out for such harsh treatment given that "today no one is put to death for avarice, hypocrisy, scurrility, or flattery, of which it is often easy to judge, but for heresy, of which it is not so simple to judge, so many are executed."[32] What is a heretic, after all? Castellio tried to arrive at a definition, but, "after careful investigation," he could "discover no more than this, that we regard those as heretics with whom we disagree."[33]

In some ways, heretics seem to be "those who are obstinate in spiritual matters and in doctrine." Thus, they are like "Hananiah, the false prophet whom Jeremiah avoided when he could not recall him from his error." But Jeremiah did no more than "predict[] to him his death in accord with the command of the Lord, not of the magistrate." This story tells us "how heretics of this sort are to be treated."[34]

Castellio also touches on the fundamentally contentious element of religious beliefs because "to judge of doctrine is not so simple as to judge of conduct." Bad conduct that is contrary to social order is easily perceived. Even "a Jew, Turk, Christian, or anyone else" can recognize that a "brigand or a traitor" is "evil and should be put to death." After all, "no controversies are raised and no books are written to prove that brigands, etc., should be put to death. This knowledge is engraved and written on the hearts of all men from the foundation of the world." Even St. Paul admitted that "the Gentiles have the law written on their hearts."[35]

Castellio thought that Christianity would stand a better chance in the "marketplace of ideas" (not his words) by softening on heresy: "Let not the Jews or Turks condemn the Christians, nor let the Christians condemn the Jews or Turks." Instead, "teach and win them by true religion and justice, and let us who are Christians, not condemn one another, but, if we are wiser than they, let us also be better and more merciful."[36] Because "who would wish to be a Christian, when he saw that those who confessed the name of Christ were destroyed by Christians themselves with fire, water, and the sword without mercy and more cruelly treated than brigands and murderers?"[37] Castellio wraps up on this point, and by making a specific, if oblique, reference to Servetus calling out to Christ from the flames:

> Who would not think Christ a Moloch, or some such god, if he wished that men should be immolated to him and burned alive? Who would wish to serve Christ on condition that a difference of opinion on a controversial point with those in authority would be punished by burning alive at the command of Christ himself more cruelly than in the bull of Phalaris even though from the midst of the flames he should call with a loud voice upon Christ, and should cry out that he believed in Him? Imagine Christ, the judge of all, present. Imagine Him pronouncing the sentence and applying the torch. Who would not hold Christ for a Satan? What more could Satan do than burn those who call upon the name of Christ?[38]

Concerning Heretics is a remarkable book that stands out as one of the most significant arguments for religious toleration of the pre-Enlightenment period. But Castellio does not argue for a modern view of religious toleration, nor does he go beyond religion and advocate for a general liberty of conscience. Jews and Turks and various Christians should not be persecuted, argues Castellio, because neither they "nor any other nations entertain a doubt whether there is but one god." Regarding monotheism, "all agree with the Christians." But Castellio's tolerance ended there. Anyone who "denies the Lord God" such as the "infidel and atheist," is "deservedly to be abhorred in the eyes of all."[39]

Similarly, although we may want to champion George of Cappadocia or Michael Servetus as martyrs for religious toleration, they were nothing of the sort. Before he fled Alexandria,

George devoted considerable energy to persecuting pagans and Trinitarian Christians. And throughout his trial at the hands of John Calvin, Servetus continually said that it should be Calvin, not he, to burn at the stake. Merely finding oneself on the losing side of a theological dispute—the side often bound to a stake—does not automatically make one a champion of religious tolerance. Thus, we discover a "recurring problem in the broader story of religious freedom, namely, that the victims of intolerance were often intolerant themselves and would not have recognized the rights of those whom they regarded as the real heretics."[40]

John Milton, a great champion of toleration, defended Protestant sects, "Lutherans, Calvinists, anabaptists, Socinians, Arminians," as groups that "may have some errors, but are no heretics." Protestants must tolerate their fellow Protestant groups because "who himself maintains the same principles, and disavows all implicit faith, would persecute, and not rather charitably tolerate, such men as these, unless he mean to abjure the principles of his own religion?" But did Milton think Catholics should be tolerated? Absolutely not. The popery "is not to be tolerated either in public or private." And if, in removing their idols, they claim "we violate their consciences," Protestants should say that "we have no warrant to regard conscience which is not grounded on Scripture."[41]

John Locke reached a high-minded conclusion in the *Essay on Toleration* (written in 1667, before the more famous *A Letter Concerning Toleration*):

> No man ought to be forced to renounce his opinion, or assent to the contrary, because such a compulsion cannot produce any real effect to that purpose for which it is designed. It cannot alter men's minds, it can only force them to be hypocrites, and by this way the magistrate is so far from bringing men to embrace the truth of his opinion, that he only constrains them to lie for their own.[42]

But would he extend that tolerance to Catholics? No. Catholics believe "doctrines absolutely destructive to the society wherein they live, as is evident in the Roman Catholics that are subjects of any prince but the pope." Because Catholics blend "such opinions with their religion," they "ought not to be tolerated by the magistrate" unless "he can allow one part, without the spreading of the other," which Locke supposed "is very hard to be done."[43]

In fact, only a few thinkers of the early Enlightenment, most notably the English Levellers and Roger Williams (the founder of Rhode Island and the subject of a chapter in this book), advocated for full, across-the-board toleration of both religious and nonreligious ideas. For these thinkers, such as Leveller William Walwyn, "no man ought to be punished for his judgment."[44]

Walwyn and his fellow Levellers stand out as some of the truly revolutionary thinkers of the Enlightenment. The group emerged during the English Revolution and criticized the lack of reforms and protections of religious liberty in the wake of Parliament's victory over the king in the civil war. John Lilburne and Richard Overton were also prominent Levellers who wrote brilliant defenses of liberty, but it was Walwyn who most skillfully advocated a broad view of toleration that exempted no religion or ideology. Moreover, Walwyn understood that comprehensive toleration would create peace and harmony among the people because so many of their problems arose from the constant attempts to impose religious commands on everyone. In his "New Petition of the Papists" (1641), Walwyn made a "humble petition" to the "afflicted brethren." His radical suggestion? Stop the madness and leave people alone:

> That whereas there are so many different Religions now professed in England; as your Honours well know, and that with griefe no doubt, casting your eyes upon the great confusion that thereby ariseth in the commonwealth; every one hoping and expecting that theirs alone shall be received and established by this present and

powefull high Court of Parliament and all others to bee cast forth abolished and prosecuted, which certainely would cause (if it be once Decreed) a farre greater confusion and discontentment.

For the timely prevention of which danger many hold it necessarie, and humbly desire, that you would take it into your deepe considerations and profound Judgements, whether it were not more convenient for this State, and more gratefull to the subjects to tollerate all professions whatsoever, every one being left to use his owne conscience, none to be punished or persecuted for it.[45]

***

Walwyn's words weren't the final pronouncement on liberty of conscience, of course, but they indicate the infancy of a radical idea that would soon become a keystone of Enlightenment liberalism. In Walwyn, we see the idea of religious toleration becoming the broader "liberty of conscience." This shift was important. Some Enlightenment thinkers actively resisted the idea of "toleration" because, to them, it implied control. To "tolerate" something implies that toleration is a gift that can be taken away. Toleration implies jurisdiction, as in the original Latin meaning, the right to "speak the laws" that must be obeyed. When the state claims jurisdiction over something, it might leave it alone, or it might change course and decide to interfere. In 1785 in *Observations on the Importance of the American Revolution, and the Means of Making It a Benefit to the World*, Richard Price wrote the following:

In Liberty of Conscience I include much more than *Toleration*. Jesus Christ has established a perfect equality among his followers. His command is, that they shall assume no jurisdiction over one another, and acknowledge no master besides *himself.*—It is, therefore, presumption in any of them to claim a right to any superiority or preeminence over their brethren, Such a claim is implied, whenever any of them pretend to *tolerate* the rest.—Not only all *Christians*, but all *men* of all religions ought to be considered by a State as equally entitled to its protection as far as they demean themselves honestly and peaceably. *Toleration* can take place only where there is a civil establishment of a particular mode of religion; that is, where a predominant sect enjoys *exclusive* advantages, and makes the encouragement of its own mode of faith and worship a part of the constitution of the State; but at the same time thinks fit to *suffer* the exercise of other modes of faith and worship. Thanks be to God, the new American States are at present strangers to such establishments. In this respect, as well as many others, they have shewn, in framing their constitutions, a degree of wisdom and liberality which is above all praise.[46]

Although the state's permitting liberty is a step in the right direction, liberalism demands more. Liberalism does not lay claim to freedom that exists only at the sufferance of the state and its agents. Liberalism is an assertion of *self*-sovereignty—a claim that the state lacks jurisdiction—over your life, your thoughts, your speech, and your property. After the seeds of liberty of conscience were established in the form of religious toleration, Enlightenment thinkers created a broader edifice of freedoms that individuals could demand as a matter of right, not as a concession. The first radical idea was to claim that unjust laws cannot be passed. The next radical idea was to say that *no* laws can be passed. In the words of historian Guido de Ruggiero:

At first, freedom of conscience is considered essential to [man's] personality; this implies religious liberty and liberty of thought. Later is added all that concerns his relations to other individuals: freedom to express and communicate his own thought, personal security against oppression, free movement, economic liberty, juridical equality, and property.[47]

In many ways, the movement from religious toleration to liberty of conscience and to the broader freedoms of property, economic liberty, and equality before the law is more important than other aspects of post-Enlightenment liberalism that are more often championed—namely, institutional innovations like democracy, republicanism, and the separation of powers. Ancient Athens had something resembling a democracy, at least for free, male citizens. Similarly, republican Rome, some medieval and Renaissance city-states (particularly in northern Italy), the Netherlands, and parts of Germany were well versed in theories of civic participation and various iterations of institutional limitations on rulers. These institutional arrangements helped provide some people in history with a "Liberty of the Ancients," in the terms of the famous taxonomy of Benjamin Constant, meaning the ability of citizens to participate in the decisionmaking of their political institutions. "Liberty of the Moderns," however, was the true innovation: establishing civil liberties, the protections of the rule of law, and broad freedoms from state interference. Indeed, Liberty of the Moderns is a direct consequence of the struggle for religious toleration.

This introduction explains why the stories of George of Cappadocia, Michael Servetus, and thousands of others who suffered for their beliefs should not be forgotten, and why the lessons that were learned from their struggles helped produce a radical new idea: freedom. Not just freedom in your thoughts and religious practices, but a broader freedom that guarantees your ability to live your life according to your conscience.

***

We live in an increasingly secular age, with religion often treated with either a sneer or outright contempt. For many, religion is an outmoded, stone-age construct that outlived any usefulness it may have once had. Better to put away childish things and move on to a worldview based on science and reason.

But every age has its pieties, its ideas that cannot be challenged without encountering contempt, shouts, insults, and occasionally the pitchfork-bearing mob or, as is increasingly the case today, the sign-waving, belligerent college student. Despite emerging from the struggles of freethinkers who tried to live their lives according to their consciences, modern "liberalism" too often resembles the inquisitors that their laudable progenitors once resisted.

We seem to be locked in an unending cycle: those who once asked for tolerance become intolerant when they acquire power. Modern "freethinkers," often atheists and secularists, demand that Christian bakers be forced to bake for same-sex weddings, that Christian businesses be forced to provide abortifacient contraceptives to their employees, and that Christian children be forced to learn evolution in school. In so doing, the freethinkers betray their heritage. Those who were once burned have become the burners. But we do not burn people at the stake anymore, of course. Instead we immolate people's jobs and careers, and we pillory them on Twitter.

***

In the wake of Donald Trump's election, it has become clear that America is a deeply divided nation: red versus blue, Republican versus Democrat, Christian versus atheist. We fight, a lot. But, historically, it was in times of intense conflict between ideologically divided people that calls for religious toleration and liberty of conscience were most needed. The Thirty-Years War was an unimaginably bloody conflict that arose largely from attempts to impose religious doctrines on the unwilling. The resulting Peace of Westphalia was a type of toleration, a truce that let countries pursue their own religious goals. The English Civil War was likewise partially rooted in conflicts between Catholics and Protestants, and it was during that tumultuous decade that the wisdom of the Levellers was most needed. William Walwyn knew that liberty of conscience was the only way to find peace between the warring factions:

> It may be objected that this Tolleration would breede a
> greater confusion, but wee which know wee have the

Spirit, beleeve the contrary; for the establishing of onely one, and suppressing all others, will breede, in all a generall discontent, jarring, rayling, libelling, and consequently must needs follow a mighty confusion, where contrarywise, if all were permitted, all would bee pleased all in peace, and their obligation and love would be farre greater to the King and State for so great a benefit as the freedome of conscience, which to all men is the most gratefull thing in the world.[48]

Toleration and liberty of conscience is one method—perhaps, ultimately, the only method—by which people with deep commitments to different values can live together cooperatively rather than combatively. Given our national discord, perhaps it is time to re-learn the history and the ideas that I have briefly and imperfectly summarized here and that are further discussed in the pages that follow.

Now, more than ever, the ideas of religious toleration and liberty of conscience should not be put to the flames.

2. Opening Essay: Protecting Religious Liberty in the Culture Wars

Douglas Laycock

For several years now, I have been urging the two sides in America's culture wars to respect the liberty of the other side: to concentrate on protecting their own liberty and to spend much less time on—indeed to mostly give up on—regulating the liberty of their opponents.[1] These fights are not just about sex, but they are heavily about sex. I have long warned of the Puritan mistake.[2] The Puritans came to Massachusetts for religious liberty and immediately established that they meant religious liberty only for themselves. Anyone else had the liberty to go anywhere in the world outside Massachusetts, and that was quite enough liberty for the likes of them.

I'm more practical than most academics; I do argue cases in the courts. But on this plea for mutual tolerance, I'm an utterly impractical and academic voice crying in the wilderness. No one on either side has paid me the slightest mind. But I'll try once more, maybe to a friendlier audience.

It hasn't always been this way. We Americans haven't always been so intolerant. The Religious Freedom Restoration Act (RFRA) passed in 1993 with bipartisan support. The sponsors in the Senate were Orrin Hatch and Ted Kennedy. It passed 97–3 in the Senate and unanimously in the House. Bill Clinton signed it with enthusiasm. But that's not the only way in which things were different.

Why did it take three and a half years from the Supreme Court's decision in *Employment Division v. Smith* to pass a bill that had overwhelming bipartisan support?[3] The opposition came from the right. It came from the Catholic bishops and the more paranoid elements of the pro-life movement, who were afraid that the Religious Freedom Restoration Act was really the Abortion Restoration Act in disguise. In those days, it was widely anticipated on both left and right that the Supreme Court would soon overrule *Roe v. Wade*.[4] Some members of the pro-life movement became convinced that women would just say that their abortion was religiously motivated. They also believed the Supreme Court would take a political hit for overturning *Roe* and so would turn around and find a new right to abortion under RFRA. It never made much sense, but it held up the bill for three and a half years.[5]

Two things finally made the opposition go away. One was *Planned Parenthood v. Casey*,[6] which more or less reaffirmed *Roe*; the other was the election of Bill Clinton. If George H. W. Bush had been reelected, there would not have been a Religious Freedom Restoration Act. It was essential not only that *Roe v. Wade* be reaffirmed, but also that the pro-life movement give up—at least for the time—on the prospect of appointing the fifth vote.

The world was very different 23 years ago with respect to these issues. Because the opposition to RFRA came from the right, the hearing testimony was aimed at the right. When people tried to explain why this bill was needed, they said things like, "the gay rights groups are trying to make the Catholic schools hire gay teachers," and "the pro-choice groups are trying to make Catholic hospitals perform abortions." Both of those things were true. Not as true as they are now, but both those things were true. I testified to that, and Nadine Strossen, the president of the American Civil Liberties Union (ACLU), also testified to that.[7]

RFRA was enacted unanimously because there was very broad support for the principle of religious liberty. The coalition was wall-to-wall, it was left and right, it was religious and secular.[8] The National Association of Evangelicals was part of it, the Church of Jesus Christ of Latter-Day Saints was part of it, the ACLU was part of it, and People for the American Way was part of it. All the major Jewish groups were part of it. All those groups disagreed on many things. They disagreed on which government interests were sufficiently compelling to override religious liberty, and they knew they would be in court against each other once this bill was passed. But they agreed on the principle of the thing: government should not burden the exercise of religion without a compelling reason.

Fast-forward five or six years to 1998–1999 and the debates on the Religious Liberty Protection Act (RLPA).[9] After the Supreme Court struck down RFRA as applied to the states, Congress tried to replace it to the extent possible under the commerce power and the spending power. That bill died principally because gay rights groups demanded a carve-out of all civil rights claims, and they united the civil rights community behind them.[10]

That argument was what killed the bill. But lots of other points were argued along the way. A couple of law professors claimed the bill would be unconstitutional because it exceeded the scope of the commerce power, and it was an abuse of the spending power, and it violated separation of powers. There were about 15 constitutional arguments against it. The Democratic minority report in the House Committee on Civil and Constitutional Rights stated the bill was unconstitutional for reasons that would have cast constitutional doubt on everything since the New Deal.[11] Cato would have loved it. And you know the Democrats who signed that report didn't believe a word of it. But it was an attempt to kill this bill because it didn't have a civil rights carve-out.

Rep. Jerrold Nadler (D-NY) offered an amendment to carve out most but not quite all civil rights claims.[12] He would have allowed a religious liberty defense to housing discrimination claims within the scope of the narrow exception of the federal Fair Housing Act (four units or fewer, one of which is owner-occupied). He would have allowed an exception to employment discrimination claims for employers with five or fewer employees. He would not have allowed any religious liberty defense to public accommodation claims. That wasn't much, but it's more than is on the table now. I'm not sure any Democrat would agree to those proposals today. The Nadler Amendment was defeated in a vote that was heavily partisan but not entirely along party lines. A significant number of conservative or moderate Democrats and more liberal or moderate Republicans crossed party lines in that vote.[13] That was in 1999.

Today, state religious freedom restoration acts are politically toxic. Think of the dramatic reaction to the Indiana legislation. But the same arguments in somewhat less-fevered forms are made with respect to any religious liberty bill these days. Democrats oppose religious liberty. Republicans support religious liberty—mostly for the wrong reasons, and not including Muslims and other groups that they don't really approve of. Sen. Strom Thurmond (R-SC) proposed an amendment to RLPA to exclude Wiccans from military bases. And we had to explain to him that the one thing that is clearly unconstitutional, even under the narrowest reading of the Supreme Court's rule, is singling out a particular group by name and subjecting its members to a special disability.[14] That was still unconstitutional, so his amendment wouldn't accomplish anything. And we continue to have that issue with people who support religious liberty mostly for religions very much like their own.

Some of the claims that were made in the hysteria over the Indiana RFRA were really quite remarkable.[15] "It would be a license to discriminate" was the most common and, actually, among the mildest. "A state RFRA would allow anti-Semites to refuse to serve Jews. It feels very much like a prelude to a new Kristallnacht"—that is a real quotation. Maybe the most extreme complaint came in response to the proposed Michigan RFRA, which was not enacted: "It would allow emergency medical technicians to refuse treatment to gay patients." Of course, it's hard to imagine any medical provider taking that position. But if you understand your opponents to be hateful bigots, then you can impute anything to them. More important, if there is anything that is clearly, indisputably, a compelling interest, it's emergency medical care.

The people who claim exemptions these days are vilified, sometimes boycotted, sometimes defamed on Yelp and other review sites, sometimes vandalized. All of those things happened to Sweetcakes by Melissa, the baker in Oregon who declined to make a wedding cake for a same-sex couple. The business is now closed.[16]

Now, if you look at some of the recent litigation, the interest groups on the two sides line up with their tribes without making any distinctions, either supporting or opposing the religious liberty claim. (There are a very few exceptions, and I'll come back to them). If you look at the two contraception cases, *Hobby Lobby*[17] and *Zubik*,[18] it seems to me that there is a fundamental difference between the two cases. The difference is not necessarily dispositive and would not necessarily persuade everybody, but it is a difference that I think would persuade a significant number of people (that is, if anyone were persuadable). Hobby Lobby had to contract for and pay for drugs that it believed caused abortions. Bishop Zubik and the Little Sisters of the Poor do not have to pay for anything they object to, they don't have to contract for anything they object to, and they don't have to arrange for anything they object to. That difference seems pretty dramatic. But except for me and the Baptist Joint Committee for Religious Liberty,[19] it doesn't seem to have made a shred of difference to anybody. It did not appear to make a difference to anybody on the Court, and, except for the Baptist Joint Committee, it didn't make a difference to any of the amici curiae filing on the two sides.

If you look at what was going on in Congress in June 2016, all the appropriations bills were frozen because of two amendments. The Russell Amendment said that government contractors keep the right to hire on the basis of religion if they are a religious organization. The amendment reaches no further than that; it's confined to religious organizations—religious nonprofits—that have government contracts.[20] The Maloney Amendment said that all government contractors are subject to President Barack Obama's 2014 executive order (which bars federal contractors from discriminating on the basis of sexual orientation or gender identity),[21] which is, in fact, ambiguous. I don't think the Maloney Amendment does what its supporters think it does. In September, Rep. Sean Patrick Maloney (D-NY) was demanding that the president veto the entire defense appropriations bill if the Russell Amendment language was not removed.[22]

The key point here is that no public statement that I've seen from either side, Republican or Democratic, suggests that there's the slightest conflict of values here, the slightest difficulty, or anything to figure out. My side is right. No, my side is right. You are suppressing religious liberty. You are legislating discrimination. Neither side sees any issue; each side cares only about its own interest group.

The *New York Times*'s coverage of religious freedom restoration acts now puts religious freedom in scare quotes, or it says "so-called religious freedom bills," or it does both in the same sentence.[23] The *Times* may think these laws go too far. It may think they're a bad idea. It may oppose religious liberty, or oppose religious liberty in the context of gay rights. But these laws are not some other category. Whether wise or foolish, they *are* religious freedom bills. That isn't "so-called"; that's what they do.

The civil libertarian position is to protect the rights of both sides to the greatest extent possible. But the ACLU at the national level has gone entirely over to one side. It sees a hierarchy of rights. Religious liberty is still one the ACLU cares about, but it's at the bottom of the list. If it conflicts in any way with anything else the ACLU cares about, it loses.[24] And at the state and local level— the ACLU is a very decentralized organization—local units often actively oppose any kind of religious exemption.

All this is very sad. We tell our children that America offers liberty and justice for all. That includes religious minorities. That includes religious minorities on both sides: conservative believers as well as atheists and agnostics. And it certainly should include sexual minorities. Religious and sexual minorities make essentially parallel claims on the larger society. They say that some aspects of human identity are so fundamental that they should be left to each individual, free from all nonessential regulation. Sexual orientation is that fundamental, and for many religious believers, religion is that fundamental. Each of those identities is routinely manifested in conduct. It is wholly unreasonable to expect gays and lesbians to remain celibate all their lives. It is equally unreasonable to expect religious believers not to act according to their understanding of God's will. Each side understands that idea for themselves, but they do not understand it for the other side. Moreover, each side seeks to live out its identity in public, not in the closet. Believers practice their faith in their churches, in their charitable works, in their jobs and businesses, and in their public lives.[25]

And each side is viewed as evil by a substantial portion of the population. Religious conservatives think that gays and lesbians are committed to a life of immoral and disordered conduct. Gays and lesbians and their supporters think that religious conservatives are hateful bigots. Each side indulges poorly informed stereotypes about the other. Consequently, each side is vulnerable to biased and unreasonable regulations in jurisdictions where the other side can muster a majority. These minorities are not exactly discrete and insular—though there's some of that—but they are certainly the subject of bias and prejudice.[26]

What would it look like to try to protect the rights and liberties of both sides? Women are entitled to reproductive health care. Gays and lesbians are entitled to marriage, to weddings. Very occasionally, only the conscientious objector can provide those things, but there aren't many cases like that. There are some. There are cases of local monopolies in rural areas and small towns. There are cases of emergency medical treatment. But for the most part, we can exempt conscientious objectors without inflicting tangible harm on the women seeking reproductive care and on the gays and lesbians seeking to marry and otherwise live their lives. The market will respond; there are plenty of other providers.[27]

So the real issue is the dignitary harm. Advocates for gays and lesbians and women in need of reproductive care say, "We are insulted. We are offended. It is terrible when a doctor or a merchant tells us 'I can't do what you're asking me to do because I think it's wrong. I think it's sinful, and I can't be part of it.'" They are insulted and offended, and that's a real harm.

I don't want to minimize that harm, but I want to note some important things about it. It does not outweigh the harm of violating conscience. On the religious side, the conscientious objector who is forced to provide medical treatment that he believes immoral, or is forced to participate in a religious ceremony that he believes violates God's law, disrupts his relationship with God. For many religious believers, that is the most important relationship in their lives. And for some of them, they believe the disruption is permanent. Viewed in purely secular terms, there is emotional harm on both sides of the balance.[28]

We can take the argument a step further. The offended gay couples who have to find another wedding planner still get to live their own lives by their own values. The regulated believer who is forced to close her business or to assist in same-sex marriages does not get to live her own life by her own values. Thus, first, the harm of regulation on the religious side is greater than the dignitary or insult harm on the secular side.

Second, this kind of insult or offense has been held not to be a compelling government interest in the free speech context. Few things are better settled than the principle that government cannot censor speech because it is offensive. Think about *Cohen v. California*[29]—the "Fuck the Draft" case—or *Hurley v. Irish-American*

Gay, Lesbian, and Bisexual Group of Boston[30]—the case about the parade that excluded gay and lesbian groups from marching. Those cases were about *speech*. The wedding planner who doesn't want to do a same-sex wedding is engaged in *conduct*. But in many jurisdictions (32 now, arguably 33 jurisdictions), the right to practice your religion free of government-imposed burdens is protected by heightened judicial review—in most of those jurisdictions, by the compelling government interest test.[31] An insult or offense is not a compelling government interest under settled constitutional law with respect to free speech. Neither should it be a compelling interest in those jurisdictions that have rejected *Smith* and protected religious conduct with a compelling government interest standard.

Is there any way to protect the liberty of both sides? What we obviously need but cannot achieve are strong gay rights laws, a strong doctrine on reproductive health care, and strong religious exemptions for both. It's too late for that in blue states. Gay rights laws are already in place, and the religious side has no remaining leverage to bargain with.

But there's an obvious deal to be done in Congress and in red states going forward. A slight majority of American jurisdictions still do not have a gay rights law. If we're going to enact gay rights laws in Alabama or Tennessee or other red or reddish-purple states, they're going to have to have religious exemptions. That's why the gay rights side is trying to bypass the legislative bargaining process by reinterpreting Title VII and Title IX to apply not only to sex discrimination but also to sexual-orientation discrimination.[32] If that happens, and it might, then bargaining will be impossible.

The more alluring possibility, at least for now, is the nationwide or statewide grand bargain in Congress or in red states. We can prohibit discrimination against gays and lesbians and provide strong and effective remedies *if* the bill has appropriate and adequate exemptions for conscientious objectors, at least in religious contexts such as weddings. The problem with that solution is the problem with any legislative compromise: Republicans oppose the anti-discrimination law, Democrats oppose the religious exemption, and many on both sides would rather have no bill at all than accept the part of the bill that they oppose. And what I hear from people on Capitol Hill is that there's just not much support. Neither side is the least bit interested in compromise. Both sides want to crush the other.

Utah is the shining example, but it's also a discouraging story when you look more closely. It is now illegal in Utah, the reddest state in the country, to discriminate in employment or housing on the basis of sexual orientation or sexual identity.[33] That's a huge accomplishment. Churches, the Boy Scouts, religious nonprofits, and their affiliates and subsidiaries are wholly exempt. Small employers are exempt. And the new law does not cover public accommodations, so it hasn't solved that problem. It's far from a complete deal, but it's a very important deal. It was made possible by the leadership of the Mormon Church (which can speak for most religious conservatives in the state), several key legislators, and, I'm told, a personal relationship between a gay legislator and a conservative Republican legislator.

The Utah deal was immediately denounced by the gay rights community nationwide and by some scholars.[34] They said it's not a model for anywhere else; it's only in Utah. They oppose exemptions now even for religious nonprofits. We're past the *Hobby Lobby* issue about whether business corporations are different. Now we're told that not even religious nonprofits should get exemptions from gay rights laws. On the other side, I understand that some Republican legislators in Utah—not most, but some— hate the deal and feel they gave away too much. So elements on both sides hate it. That's usually the sign of a good compromise. But it also shows the difficulty of doing such a deal anywhere else.

My comments have been pessimistic so far, but let me say a couple things about how the glass is maybe a quarter full. In the past 10 years, there have been three unanimous wins for the free exercise of religion in the Supreme Court of the United States. How in the world did that happen in this time of polarization?

First was *Gonzales v. O Centro Espirita Beneficente Uniao do Vegetal,*[35] about a small group in Santa Fe—an offshoot of a much larger group in Brazil—that uses a hallucinogenic tea from the Brazilian jungle in its worship service. The case was decided for the religious group by an 8–0 Supreme Court; it would have been a 9–0 win if either Justice Sandra Day O'Connor or Justice Samuel Alito could have voted.

Hosanna-Tabor Evangelical Lutheran Church and School v. EEOC said that courts will not second-guess decisions of churches and religious organizations about the employment of their religious leadership.[36] No one who heard that oral argument thought that it would garner a 9–0 or even 6–3 vote, but it turned out to be 9–0. And *Holt v. Hobbs* held that a Muslim prisoner could wear a short beard in the Arkansas state prisons.[37]

Two of those cases, *O Centro* and *Holt v. Hobbs,* had no interest that liberals care about. There was no reason for left-leaning public-interest civil-liberties organizations to oppose a group that wanted to get ever-so-slightly high at its worship service and no reason to support the oppressive prison administration in Arkansas.

The same can't really be said about *Hosanna-Tabor.* That was an employment discrimination case, and, of course, liberal interest groups and the liberal justices care about employment discrimination. But *Hosanna-Tabor* was employment discrimination within the context of the church itself, and the lower courts had been unanimous for 40 years,[38] which doesn't happen very often. I think the reason judges have been so often unanimous is that, when they contemplate the kinds of issues they would have to decide if they started reviewing employment discrimination claims by ministers, they don't want any part of it—and for good reason. And their intuition about the difficulties they would face as judges is congruent with the reason the religion clauses protect the right of churches, synagogues, and mosques to choose their own religious leadership.

Those three cases tell us that, if there's no opposing interest that progressives care about, we can still come together and generate broad support for religious liberty. But as soon as any other interest that progressives care about comes into play, the religious liberty claim generally loses. That's the situation we're in, and that betrays progressive ideals. Anyone who cares about the rights of both sides is now perceived as centrist at best and an oddball at worst. My roots are on the left. I'm an old-style William Brennan secular, civil libertarian. I think we can do better than the record I have just reviewed. I think we can protect the liberty of both sides.

Now let me just say one more word about the Obama administration, which was often attacked for being on the anti-religious side of these issues. I think that's just not true. The Obama administration had a mixed record, and a couple times I think they were seriously wrong. Their initial position on contraception was a mistake. I think their ultimate position was quite defensible and offers a substantial solution to religious conscientious objectors. I think their litigating position on *Hosanna-Tabor*—they said there shouldn't be a ministerial exception—was clearly a mistake. I don't think that came from the White House; I think it came from the Equal Employment Opportunity Commission and the Justice Department. They had a case that wound up in the Supreme Court, and they didn't think they could win on whether the plaintiff was a minister. So they were forced into an all-or-nothing position. But wherever that choice came from, and whatever the reasons, I think it was a mistake.

However, the Obama administration was terrific about enforcing the Religious Land Use and Institutionalized Persons Act (RLUIPA).[39] They appeared in courts around the country. They brought their own cases, and they filed amicus briefs in support of private cases. And as I said, the currently proposed but still in litigation solution to the contraception battle is a good solution. At the very least, even if you think it's inadequate, it is not a war-on-religion position. It's a position that goes a long way toward trying to accommodate the religious objection.

The Obama administration also very quietly left in place a George W. Bush executive order that says a religious organization that gets a government grant or contract does not thereby forfeit its Title VII right to hire on the basis of religion.[40] And it quietly left in place a Bush-era opinion of the Office of Legal Counsel that says RFRA applies to government grants.[41] An organization that gets a government grant may have an RFRA claim about religiously burdensome conditions imposed on that grant. And the administration adhered to those positions despite intense and persistent pressure to withdraw that executive order and that opinion—pressure from Democratic legislators and from organizations that represent their base.[42]

I think the administration got the religious liberty issue wrong in *Town of Greece v. Galloway*.[43] They filed a brief defending the right of the majority to impose Christian prayer rituals on citizens of other faiths and of none. But the folks who accuse the administration of a war on religion certainly aren't complaining about that. That's a pro-religion win for those folks, because the religion they mostly or exclusively care about is their own.

So in some ways the Obama administration was heroic on religious liberty, and in some ways not so good. But conservatives should not believe their own rhetoric about the administration. The things the administration did to support religious liberty are a sign that the glass is at least partially full. The news is not all bad.

Still, the level of polarization is bad. The lack of respect for any rights of the other side is bad. Both sides in the culture wars seem to be equally intolerant of the other. And these attitudes make it very difficult to protect religious liberty. A First Amendment right should not be a partisan, party-line issue, but religious liberty is in great danger of becoming just that.

SECTION I:

THE PHILOSOPHY AND HISTORY OF RELIGIOUS LIBERTY

3. The Opening Argument: Church, State, and the Birth of Liberty

John M. Barry

The question of church and state is probably—not probably—*is* the oldest argument in American history. It was first articulated almost 400 years ago by John Winthrop, the most important figure in the early Massachusetts Bay Colony. Winthrop gave what the *New York Times* called the greatest sermon in the last 1,000 years, which included the famous phrase, "We shall be as a city upon a hill."[1] His definition of Americans as a new chosen people has informed American culture ever since.

But, from the very beginning, there was an alternative vision, articulated by Roger Williams, a Puritan minister whom Winthrop himself described as "godly." Williams was so respected that, upon his arrival in Boston, Winthrop offered him the ministry of the Boston church, the greatest such post in America. Williams declined because he considered that church not pure enough for him. Yet Williams envisioned a very different kind of city on a hill: a city where church and state were utterly separate, a city where citizens had individual freedom in a way approaching how we understand it today.

The dispute between Winthrop and Williams defined, for the first time, two fault lines that have run through American history ever since. The first fault line is obvious: the proper relation between what man has made of God—that is, the church—and the state. The second is more subtle: the proper relation between a free individual and the state, the shape of liberty.

Understanding the development of these fault lines involves intellectual history, but the fault lines themselves and the ideas that Williams articulated—and eventually the First Amendment—did not come from any intellectual exercise. They did not come from theory. They were specific responses to specific historic events. Those events led eventually to the beheading of an archbishop, to civil war, to the beheading of a king, and to a revolution 100 years before ours. I'd like to talk about these events and their relationship to theory.

***

The history I want to review began upon Queen Elizabeth's death in 1603, when King James VI of Scotland became King James I of England. He immediately made many people anxious by attacking both England's body and soul.

He attacked the soul like this: in 1603, there were people who could remember in their own lifetimes that, under Henry, England had been Catholic, then became Protestant. Under Henry's daughter Mary it became Catholic again, and under Elizabeth I it became Protestant again. Each of those regimes had persecuted, imprisoned, and executed dissenters, even burning them at the stake. James was nominally Protestant, but the reformers in the Church of England distrusted his commitment to the Protestant faith. Both his parents were Catholics, he married his child to a Catholic, and he began pushing the Church of England closer and closer to Catholic forms of worship. And, although Catholics attempted to assassinate him—the Gunpowder Plot would have blown up both him and Parliament—James ceased persecuting them and began to apply to Protestant dissenters laws originally aimed at Catholics. Of Puritans, he said he would "harry them out of this land or worse, hang them, that's all."

He also attacked the body of England. In Scotland, he had exercised much more power than English tradition and law allowed, and he edged the English monarchy toward absolute power, injecting the concept of the divine right of kings—which had not previously existed in England—into English jurisprudence. His apologists said, "At his coronation he took an oath not to alter the laws of the land, yet this oath notwithstanding he may alter or suspend any particular law that seemeth hurtful to the public estate."[2] Even more definitively, James's apologists claimed, "The king is the law speaking."[3]

Enter Sir Edward Coke (pronounced "cook"). Coke is arguably the greatest jurist in English history. First, as chief justice of the Court of Common Pleas, and then, as chief justice of the King's Bench, Coke in effect organized the common law in his writings by assembling and interpreting past precedents. He also set hugely important precedents, including judicial review of legislative acts and no double jeopardy in criminal trials. Perhaps most important, he pioneered the use of habeas corpus in a form we are familiar with today. Previously, the writ had been used to expand the crown's power: the crown would demand that some distant lord who had arbitrarily imprisoned someone show what law of the king the prisoner had violated. Coke issued habeas corpus writs against the crown. A believer in equality before the law and limits on state power, he issued his most famous ruling in slightly different language on several occasions: "The house of every man is as his castle."

He also had great personal courage. When the king claimed to be above the law and the protector of the law, he told the king to his face that the law was above the king and that the law protected the king. When James removed him from the bench and threw him into the Tower of London, Coke continued his defiance, saying, "If the king desires my head, he knows where he may find it." Eventually released from the tower, he led the opposition to the crown in the Parliament.

Accompanying Coke to several confrontations with James, to the Star Chamber, to court, was a brilliant young amanuensis with whom Coke was so taken that he referred to him as "my son" and sent him to the best preparatory school in England. The boy was

Roger Williams. From his years with Coke, Williams absorbed a deep understanding of liberty, state power, and the law—and not the law as in any specific court ruling or legislative act but the very concept of law, as a kind of infrastructure around which society organizes itself. Decades after Coke's death, Williams referred to his "much honored friend, that man of honor, and wisdom, and piety. . . . How many thousand times since I had the honorable and precious remembrance of his person, and the life, the writings, the speeches, and the example of that glorious light."[4]

Francis Bacon influenced Williams as well. This was ironic because, although Bacon is today known as the father of the scientific method, he was then King James I's chief apologist and served James as attorney general and chancellor of England. (Incidentally, Thomas Hobbes was Bacon's secretary.) Bacon and Coke despised each other, tried to destroy each other, and essentially succeeded in doing so. Bacon convinced James to remove Coke from the bench and throw him into the Tower. Upon his release, Coke convinced Parliament to impeach Bacon, the first impeachment in 150 years. It is a sign of Williams's independence of thought that, although Coke was this great father figure, he was actually willing to learn from Bacon, rejecting Bacon's politics but absorbing a scientific methodology—that is, the idea of testing hypotheses. Indeed, Williams cites Bacon in the dedication of his most important book, and Coke's name does not appear until page two.

When James's son Charles became king, Charles intensified the pressure on both religious and political dissenters. One clergyman—whose enmity to Puritans made him a favorite of the king—wrote, "Before God, it will never be well until we have our Inquisition."[5] In politics, Charles began usurping even more power than his father. As Charles pressed ever harder both on religious dissenters and on the historic rights and privileges of Parliament and England, one parliamentary leader said he had wanted to "postpone the business of religion" to focus on "our rights," but "never was there a more clear connection between the matter of religion and matter of state."[6]

Parliament challenged the king on both fronts. Coke led the response. In 1628, he wrote the Petition of Right, which placed explicit limits on the crown and includes several of the amendments in our Bill of Rights as well as the habeas corpus clause in the U.S. Constitution. He then ushered it through both the House of Commons and the House of Lords—both passed it unanimously—and forced Charles to accept it.

But Charles railed against the restrictions placed upon him and soon began ignoring them. Parliament protested—violently. In a chaotic scene, while soldiers stormed the doors to adjourn Parliament upon the king's order, Parliament passed resolutions declaring capital enemies—traitors—those who supported some of the king's policies. When soldiers finally broke in, leading members of Parliament fled or were arrested. Williams—then a trusted messenger between members who opposed Charles—witnessed all this from the gallery.

Soon after, England would explode in civil war, and Parliament would not meet again for 11 years—not until Charles was desperate. Meanwhile, to escape the boiling political tensions and ever-increasing persecution, thousands of Puritans fled to America—including, of course, Winthrop and Williams.

***

As governor of Massachusetts, Winthrop was determined to build a New Jerusalem to advance the glory of God. God informed every aspect of life in Massachusetts, including the legal code. Although Winthrop himself had been a prominent attorney in England, this legal code was not written by lawyers but by ministers (its first draft was called "Moses His Judicialls"). One of the Bay's leading ministers said the plantation would "endeavour after a Theocracy as near as might be to that which was the glory of Israel."[7] Colonists had to conform to God's will, as interpreted by the colony's ministers and magistrates. Conformity went beyond merely obeying the law. Winthrop believed in liberty but in "a liberty to do only that which is good," to be maintained by "subjection to authority." Colony leaders pressured all to conform, to join and participate in the community. Becoming a full-fledged church member was an arduous process, but church attendance was mandatory even for nonmembers. No individual was to stand alone; indeed, the colony prohibited individuals, even unmarried adult men, from living alone.

Like Winthrop, Williams also wanted a godly society, but from the very first he disagreed with basing law on scripture or using government to compel any aspect of worship. His views evolved gradually, but the essence of his position was present when he opposed a requirement that colonists take an oath of loyalty to the government of Massachusetts—and very pointedly not to the king.

For Williams, requiring an oath, an act of worship, mixed church and state. He knew that when you mix religion and politics you get politics, and politics inevitably corrupted the church. (Actually, when you mix anything with politics you get politics.) His position derived not only from Coke's views on liberty, that each man's home was his castle—views that ran in his veins—but even more from scripture itself and from a recognition of human error. A linguist, Williams read scripture in many languages and recognized differences between translations. To decide which meaning was correct, which interpretation of a passage was correct, required a human to make a judgment regarding God. And all humans made errors.

Because of the possibility of human error, because humans had to interpret God's word, it followed that no one should force his or her possibly erroneous interpretation upon another. To do so was, in Williams's words, "monstrous partiality." For the state to use its power to do so was unconscionable. He concluded that only total and complete separation of church and state stopped the corruption of the church and prevented forcing someone to accept error. So he rejected the idea that the state had power to insert itself between humans and god.

He also argued that the parable in the Gospel of Matthew on separating wheat and tares meant that the state should make no effort to force conformity to any doctrine or practice.[8] To Williams, that parable meant that error should be allowed to exist; in contrast, Augustine had interpreted the identical passage as justifying death to heretics and blasphemers.

Williams was a minister in Salem, Massachusetts, widely respected for both religiosity and scholarship, and his views began to get traction in the colony. He became a threat to order. There was no theological difference between him and either other ministers or the Puritan government, but there was a vast difference in their views of the state's role. Massachusetts magistrates ordered him not to "preach publicly on these matters" (which should remind us of why the First Amendment links freedom of religion and freedom of speech—it doesn't do you much good to think freely if you can't speak those thoughts). Williams refused to obey, so Massachusetts authorities banished him for his "dangerous errors," sent soldiers from Boston to arrest him, and put him on a ship returning to England.

Persecution in England was then at its height; deportation meant a certain prison sentence, probably for life, after mutilation. Another man whose criticism of the Church of England was less extreme than Williams's was sentenced to a life term, not to begin until after he was tied to a stake to receive 36 lashes, placed in the pillory for two hours, branded in the face with "SS" for "Sower of Sedition," then had his nose split and his ears cut off. Reportedly, upon hearing the sentence, William Laud, the Archbishop of Canterbury, threw his cap in the air and gave thanks to God.

Winthrop—who supported banishing Williams but opposed returning him to England to face such a sentence—sent him a warning of what was to happen. Williams immediately fled, into the teeth of a blizzard. Through the winter, Indians kept him alive. In the spring, he founded Providence. His ideas were still not fully developed, but he expressed their essence in a very simple document: the governing compact of Providence.

Every other founding document in the New World—whether Portuguese, Spanish, English, French, Dutch, Swedish, or other— said that the colony was founded to glorify God, to carry out God's will, to spread Christianity, or something to that effect. However, a draft of the compact that would govern Providence only asked for God's blessing—and in the final version of the compact, Williams deleted even that. The compact made no mention of divinity at all. This was extraordinary not only for the times, but also for Williams personally. In practically every paragraph of his own writing, he quotes scripture or refers to God. But the Providence government was to be only civil, and it would not compel anyone to any belief. Therefore, Williams concluded that there should be no mention of God. Williams's colony was to be a place where the soul was free, and he began speaking about "soul liberty." In 1652, Rhode Island actually outlawed slavery, making it probably the freest place in the world.

So how much influence did Williams have? He is a very controversial figure. Some historians—including Edmund Morgan, probably our greatest colonial historian—consider him a precursor to everyone from Thomas Paine to Thomas Jefferson and even Andrew Jackson. Others consider him *de minimis*. William McLoughlin called him "a magnificent failure . . . because of the inability of Rhode Islanders to shape . . . the destiny of New England or the other colonies."[9]

But Williams's ideas did shape other colonies. Ironically, that influence came about chiefly because Massachusetts regarded Rhode Island as a *pestilence* on its border, a foul corruption that might infest it with error, and so tried to crush it.

To protect Rhode Island, Williams returned twice to England, to revolutionary London, a place where a king had been beheaded, a place of such intellectual ferment it was called "the world turned upside down," a place where they were defining the world anew. There he sought and eventually won protection for Rhode Island from the only person in the world that Massachusetts feared: Oliver Cromwell.

In fact, Williams spent several years in London and became a major figure there, counting not only Cromwell but also such men as John Milton and Henry Vane as friends, and moving in their circles. While there, his views matured. His ideas were not entirely without precedent. There had been the Anabaptists, there had been Sebastian Castellio, there was Hugo Grotius. Williams knew all the precedents, and he filtered the knowledge of them through his experiential understanding of the law and power, then combined all of it in a new way and took his conclusions further than anyone in his century.

He wrote numerous pamphlets and books; the most important was *The Bloudy Tenent of Persecution*, one of the most comprehensive arguments ever written for separation of church and state but also for individual freedom.[10] Literally hundreds of books and pamphlets in a five-year period directly addressed him or discussed his ideas, routinely quoting him—down to typographical errors in punctuation—but often without attribution. This was not plagiarism; it was a sign that his ideas had become so well known that they enjoyed their own existence separate from him.

And what did Williams say? He said, "Forced worship stinks in God's nostrils." He compared it to "spiritual rape." He demanded that "the most Jewish, paganist, Turkish, or anti-Christian consciences in all nations and countries" be allowed freedom to worship. He even opposed toleration, for toleration of course can be withdrawn. He argued that not only logic and evidence of the world around him (the murder of thousands of Christians by Christians for the way they worshiped Christ, the success of both Catholic and Islamic states—which proved that God did not favor those of any particular faith) but scripture, too, supported his conviction that neither church nor state had any justification for compulsion of belief.

And he made an analogy that demonstrated that, to him, church and state were wholly, entirely distinct from each other: "The Church or company of worshippers . . . is like unto a . . . Corporation, Society or Company . . . which Companies may . . . in matters concerning their Societie . . . dissent, divide, breake into Schism and Faction . . . yea wholly dissolve and breake up into pieces and yet the well-being and peace of the Citie not be in the least measure impaired or disturbed; because the essence or being of the Citie . . . is essentially distinct from those particular Societies[.]"

Although his views convinced only a minority, that minority had traction. Even Cromwell listened. When Indians got word to Williams that Massachusetts was pressuring them to convert to Christianity, for example, he convinced Cromwell to order Massachusetts to cease forced conversions of Indians.

But Williams's most revolutionary statements went beyond religion to pure politics. At the time, virtually everyone believed that the authority of government came from God. Even Parliament, in its civil war with the king, in its rejection of the divine right of kings, did not dispute that God gave the king the authority to govern. And Winthrop, after being elected governor of Massachusetts, told those who had just voted for him that "being called by you, we have our authority from God."[11]

Williams disputed this point. Since government, in his view, was entirely secular, its power could not come from God. Where, then, did it come from? "I infer that the sovereign, original, and foundation of civil power lies in the people." Those governments "have no more power, nor for no longer time, than the civil power or people consenting and agreeing shall betrust them with." Now *that* was revolutionary—particularly the concept that the governed could withdraw their consent after giving it.

Williams also said that, just as religion was utterly irrelevant to a person's performance as a soldier, physician, lawyer, ship captain, merchant, or any other civil profession, a Christian magistrate was "no more" a magistrate and no better than one "of any other Conscience or Religion."[12] Try saying that today and getting elected.

Two years after Williams left England, the Levellers were quoting him verbatim. Robert Baillie, one of his leading critics, warned that Williams's ideas would "overthrow from the very foundation the whole edifice of our civil government; no king, no Lord, must be heard of here-after; This House of Commons must be cut down, the Imperial and absolute Soveraignty must be put in the hands of the multitude of the basest people" and that Williams was "the master of our mis-orders."[13]

The restoration of the crown did not end Williams's influence; it enshrined it. Charles II decided to grant Rhode Island a royal charter that did not establish the Church of England and allowed complete freedom of worship. He called the colony his "little experiment." Charles liked the experiment so much that he included the same language about toleration in later charters for North Carolina and New Jersey, although he did establish the Church of England in those colonies. Clearly, then, Williams influenced events in other colonies.

Yet Williams's most important impact came through John Locke. While it is unlikely that many, if any, American revolutionary thinkers read Williams, they all were conversant with events in London a century earlier, and they all read Locke. And Locke was certainly familiar with Williams's work and even lived on the same estate where Williams had been a minister before he left England. Williams's influence on Locke was significant. Locke scholar and Harvard divinity school professor David Little concluded that, on the question of religious toleration, Locke's ideas are "simply restatements of the central arguments in favor of freedom of conscience developed by Roger Williams in the middle of the seventeenth century, when Locke's opinions on these subjects were being shaped."[14] Winthrop Hudson, a prominent historian of religion, observed: "The parallels with the thought of Roger Williams are so close that it is not entirely implausible conjecture to suggest that Locke's major contribution may have been to reduce the rambling, lengthy, incoherent exposition of the New England 'firebrand' to orderly, abbreviated, and coherent form. . . . It's impossible to discover a single significant difference between the arguments set forth by Williams and advanced by Locke. They scarcely differ even in the details."[15] Finally, W. K. Jordan, the president of Radcliffe and author of the classic four-volume study, *The Development of Religious Toleration in England*, concluded that not Locke's but Williams's "carefully reasoned argument for the complete dissociation of church and state was the most important contribution made during the century in this significant area of political thought."[16]

When you take this entire context into account, it becomes clear that it was no accident that our Constitution is an entirely secular document. Nowhere in it does any reference to divinity appear. It does use the word "blessing"—but it seeks the blessing not of God but of liberty. In 1797, just eight years after the Constitution was adopted, the Senate explicitly separated government from religion when it unanimously approved the Treaty of Tripoli drafted under George Washington and signed by John Adams, which stated, "The government of the United States is not in any sense founded on the Christian Religion."

There is a huge difference between a nation and a government. One can argue that the United States was founded as a Christian *nation*, which I think we were, and even that we are still a Christian nation, which I think is a little more controversial. But our government was founded upon liberty and upon the complete and absolute dissociation of church and state.

4. Religious Liberty and the Human Good

Robert P. George

Writing from a jail cell in Birmingham, Alabama, Martin Luther King, Jr., anticipated a challenge to the moral goodness of the acts of civil disobedience that landed him behind bars. He anticipated his critics asking, "How can you, Dr. King, engage in willful law breaking, when you yourself had stressed the importance of obedience to law in demanding that officials of the southern states conform to the Supreme Court's desegregation ruling in the case of *Brown v. Board of Education?*" Here is King's response to the challenge:

> The answer lies in the fact that there are two types of laws: just and unjust. I would be the first to advocate obeying just laws. One has not only a legal but a moral responsibility to obey just laws. Conversely, one has a moral responsibility to disobey unjust laws. I would agree with St. Augustine that "an unjust law is no law at all."
>
> Now, what is the difference between the two? How does one determine whether a law is just or unjust? A just law is a man-made code that squares with the moral law or the law of God. An unjust law is a code that is out of harmony with the moral law. To put it in the terms of St. Thomas Aquinas: An unjust law is a human law that is not rooted in eternal law and natural law. Any law that uplifts human personality is just. Any law that degrades human personality is unjust. All segregation statutes are

> unjust because segregation distorts the soul and damages
> the personality. It gives the segregator a false sense of su-
> periority and the segregated a false sense of inferiority.[1]

So, just laws elevate and ennoble the human personality (or, as King referred to it in other contexts, the human spirit); unjust laws debase and degrade it. His point about the morality or immorality of laws is a good reminder that what is true of "personal morality" is also true of "political morality." The choices and actions of political institutions at every level, like the choices and actions of individuals, can be right or wrong, morally good or morally bad. They can align with human well-being and fulfillment in all of its manifold dimensions; or they can fail, in any of a range of ways, to respect the integral flourishing of human beings. In many cases, when laws, policies, and institutions fail to fulfill the requirements of morality, we speak intelligibly and rightly of a violation of human rights. This is particularly true when the failure is properly characterized as an injustice—failing to honor people's equal worth and dignity; failing to give them, or even actively denying them, what they are due.

But, contrary to the teaching of the late John Rawls and the extraordinarily influential stream of contemporary liberal thought of which he was the leading exponent, I wish to suggest that good is prior to right and, indeed, to rights. Here is what I mean: to be sure, human rights, including the right to religious liberty, are among the moral principles that demand respect from all of us, including governments and international institutions (which are morally bound not only to respect human rights but also to protect them). To respect people, to respect their dignity, is, among other things, to honor their rights, including the right to lift up our fellow citizens and defend the right to religious freedom. Like all moral principles, however, human rights (including the right to religious liberty) are shaped, and given content, by the human goods they protect. Rights, like other moral principles, are intelligible as rational, action-guiding principles because they are entailments and, at some level, specifications of the integral directiveness or prescriptivity of principles of practical reason that directs our choosing toward what is humanly fulfilling and enriching (or, as Dr. King would say, uplifting) and away from what is contrary to our well-being as the kind of creatures we are—namely, human persons.

For example, the right to life is violated not only when one seeks the death of another as an end or a means to an end, but also when someone's death is foreseen and accepted unfairly as a side effect of one's action in pursuit of an end. In identifying and defending the right to life, it matters that human life is no mere instrumental good but is an intrinsic aspect of the good of human persons—an integral dimension of our overall flourishing. In the same way, in identifying and defending the right to religious liberty, it matters that religion is yet another irreducible aspect of human well-being and fulfillment—a basic human good.

But what is religion? In its fullest and most robust sense, religion is the human person's being in right relation to the divine—the more than merely human source or sources (if there be such) of meaning and value. Of course, even the greatest among us in the things of the spirit fall short of perfection in various ways; but in the ideal of perfect religion, a person would understand as comprehensively and deeply as possible the body of truths about spiritual things, and would fully order his or her life and share in the life of a community of faith that is ordered, in line with those truths. In the perfect realization of the good of religion, one would achieve the relationship that the divine—say, God himself, assuming for a moment the truth of monotheism—wishes us to have with Him.

Of course, different traditions of faith have different views of what constitutes religion in its fullest and most robust sense. There are different doctrines, different scriptures, different structures of authority, different ideas of what is true about spiritual things and what it means to be in proper relationship to the more than merely human sources of meaning and value that different traditions understand as divinity.

For my part, I believe that reason has a very large role to play for each of us in deciding where spiritual truth is to be found most robustly. By "reason," I mean not only our capacity for practical reasoning and moral judgment, but also our capacities for understanding and evaluating claims of all sorts: logical, historical, scientific, and so forth. But you need not agree with me about this to affirm with me that there is a distinct basic human good of religion—a good that is uniquely architectonic in shaping one's pursuit of and participation in all the basic human goods. Let us also affirm that one begins to realize and participate in this good from the moment one begins the quest to understand the more-than-merely-human sources of meaning and value and to live authentically by ordering one's life in line with one's best judgments of the truth in religious matters.

If I am right, then the existential raising of religious questions, the honest identification of answers, and the fulfilling of what one sincerely believes to be one's duties in the light of those answers are all parts of the human good of religion—a good whose pursuit is an indispensable feature of the comprehensive flourishing of a human being. If I am right, then, as Seamus Hasson—the great advocate of religious liberty—suggests, man is intrinsically and by nature a religious being (*homo religiosus*, to borrow the Latin from Eliade), and the flourishing of man's spiritual life is integral to his all-around well-being and fulfillment.

But if that is true, then respect for a person's well-being, or more simply respect for the person, demands respect for his or her flourishing as a seeker of religious truth and as a man or woman who lives in line with his or her best judgment of what is true in spiritual matters. And that, in turn, requires respect for his or her liberty in the religious quest—the quest to understand religious truth and order one's life in line with it. Because faith of any type, including religious faith, cannot be authentic—it cannot be faith—unless it is free; and respect for the person—that is to say, respect for his or her dignity as a free and rational creature—requires respect for his or her religious liberty. Thus, from the point of view of reason, and not merely from the point of view of the revealed teaching of a particular faith (though many faiths proclaim the right to religious freedom on theological and not merely philosophical ground), it makes sense to understand religious freedom as a fundamental human right.

Interestingly and tragically, in times past, and even in some places today, regard for persons' spiritual well-being has been the premise, and motivating factor, for denying religious liberty or conceiving of it in a cramped and restricted way. Before the Catholic Church embraced the robust conception of religious freedom that honors the civil right to give public witness and expression to sincere religious views (even when erroneous), in the document *Dignitatis Humanae* of the Second Vatican Council, some Catholics rejected the idea of a right to religious freedom on the theory that "only the truth has rights." The idea was that the state, under favorable conditions, should not only publicly identify itself with Catholicism as the true faith, but also forbid religious advocacy or proselytizing that could lead people into religious error and apostasy.

The mistake there was not in the premise: religion is a great human good and the truer the religion, the better for the fulfillment of the believer. That is true. The mistake was in the supposition that the good of religion was not being advanced or participated in outside the one true faith, and that it could be reliably protected and advanced by empowering agencies of the state to enforce civil restrictions on the advocacy of religious ideas. In rejecting this supposition, the Fathers of the Second Vatican Council did not embrace the idea that error has rights; they noticed, rather, that people have rights—even when they are in error. Among those rights, integral to authentic religion as a fundamental and irreducible aspect of the human good, is the right to express and even advocate for what one believes to be true about spiritual matters—even if one's beliefs are, in one way or another, less than fully sound and, indeed, even if they are false.

When I have assigned the document *Dignitatis Humanae* in courses addressing questions of religious liberty, I have always stressed to my students the importance of reading another document of the Second Vatican Council, *Nostra Aetate*, together with it. Whether one is Catholic or not, I don't think it is possible to achieve a rich understanding of the Declaration on Religious Liberty, and the developed teaching of the Catholic Church on religious freedom, without considering what the Council Fathers proclaim in the Declaration on Non-Christian Religions. In *Nostra Aetate*, the Fathers pay tribute to all that is true and holy in non-Christian faiths, noting that there is much that is good and worthy in Hinduism and Buddhism and, especially, Judaism and Islam. In so doing, they acknowledge the ways in which religion enriches, ennobles, and fulfills the human person in the spiritual dimension of his being, even when it does not include the defining content of what they believe to be religion in its fullest and most robust sense—namely, the incarnation of Jesus Christ. This is to be honored and respected, according to the Council Fathers, because the dignity of the human being requires it. Naturally, the nonrecognition of Christ as the Son of God must count for the Fathers as a falling short in the non-Christian faiths—even in the Jewish faith in which Christianity is rooted and which stands according to Catholic teaching in an unbroken and unbreakable covenant with God. In the same way, the proclamation of Christ as the Son of God must count as an error in Christianity from a Jewish or Muslim point of view. But, the Fathers teach, Judaism and Islam are not simply false and without merit (just as neither Judaism nor Islam teaches that Christianity is simply false and without merit); on the contrary, these traditions enrich the lives of their faithful in their spiritual dimensions, thus contributing vitally to their fulfillment.

Now, the Catholic Church does not have a monopoly on the natural-law reasoning I am using to explain and defend the human right to religious liberty. But it does have a deep commitment to such reasoning and long experience with it. In *Dignitatis Humanae*, the Fathers of the Second Vatican Council present a natural-law argument for religious freedom. They actually *begin* by presenting a natural-law argument and then supplement it with arguments appealing to the authority of God's revelation in sacred scripture. Key Catholic texts illustrate, through the teachings of an actual faith, how religious leaders and believers—and not just statesmen concerned with crafting national or international policy in circumstances of religious pluralism—can incorporate into their understanding of the basic human right to religious liberty, principles and arguments that are available to all men and women of sincerity and goodwill. Professor Rawls once referred to this as "our common human reason."

Of course, from the point of view of any believer, the further away one gets from the truth of faith in all its dimensions (what the council fathers refer to as "the fullness of religious life"), the less fulfillment is available. But that does not mean that even a primitive and superstition-laden faith, much less the faiths of advanced civilizations to which the Fathers refer, is utterly devoid of value, or that the people who practice such a faith have no right to religious liberty. Nor does it mean that atheists have no right to religious freedom. The fundaments of respect for the good of religion require that civil authority respect (and, in appropriate ways, even nurture) conditions or circumstances in which people can engage in sincere religious quest and live lives of authenticity reflecting their best judgments as to the truth of spiritual matters. To compel an atheist to perform acts that are premised on theistic beliefs that he cannot, in good conscience, share is to deny him the fundamental bit of the good of religion that is his—namely, living with honesty and integrity in line with his best judgments about ultimate reality. Coercing him to perform religious acts does him no good, since faith really must be free, and it dishonors his dignity as a free and rational person. The violation of liberty is worse than futile.

Of course, there are limits to this freedom. Sincere people can commit gross evil—even grave injustice—for the sake of religion. People seeking sincerely to get right with God, or the gods, or their conception of ultimate reality can do unspeakable wrongs. For the sake of the human good and the dignity of human persons as free and rational creatures—creatures who, according to Judaism and Christianity, are made in the very image and likeness of God—the presumption in favor of respecting liberty must be powerful and broad. But it is not unlimited. The great end of getting right with God cannot justify a morally bad means, even for the sincere believer. I don't doubt the sincerity of the Aztecs in practicing human sacrifice, or the sincerity of those in the history of various traditions of faith who used coercion and even torture in the cause of what they believed was religiously required. But those things are deeply wrong and need not (should not) be tolerated in the name of religious freedom. To suppose otherwise is to back oneself into the awkward position of supposing that violations of religious freedom (and other injustices of equal gravity) must be respected for the sake of religious freedom.

Still, to overcome the powerful and broad presumption in favor of religious liberty, to be justified in requiring the believer to do something contrary to his faith or forbidding the believer to do something his faith requires, political authority must meet a heavy burden. The legal test in the United States under the Religious Freedom Restoration Act is one way of capturing the presumption and burden: to justify a law that bears negatively on religious freedom, even a neutral law of general applicability must be supported by a compelling state interest and represent the least restrictive or intrusive means of protecting or serving that interest. We can debate, as a matter of American constitutional law or as a matter of policy, whether it is, or should be, up to courts or legislators to decide when exemptions to general, neutral laws should be granted for the sake of religious freedom, or to determine when the presumption in favor of religious freedom has been overcome; but the substantive matter of what religious freedom demands from those who exercise the levers of state power should be something on which reasonable people of goodwill across the religious and political spectrums should agree—precisely because it is a matter capable of being settled by our common human reason.

5. As Government Expands, So Should Religious Liberty Protections

Doug Bandow

Issues of liberty and religion—how church and state relate—are always important. Religious liberty has greater urgency these days, and people in the religious community are concerned, because they're seeing challenges to their faith that they hadn't seen in the past. The historical context of religious liberty issues is worth considering as we look at the changes around us.

Religious liberty has been called the first freedom. It played an especially important role in early America, which was filled with European transplants fleeing various forms of religious tyranny. Of course, a number of those coming to America were willing to coerce others when given the opportunity. Nevertheless, the First Amendment showed real genius in attempting to simultaneously protect the free exercise of religion and bar government establishment of religion. But it necessarily creates a tension in practice, and we live with that tension even today.

In the early days, government rules on religion had limited impact, primarily because the federal government was quite limited. The First Amendment originally applied only to the national government, and the national government didn't do an awful lot. So God was kept out of public affairs because most public affairs were fairly minor. If you were going to be salt and light, as Jesus enjoined his believers as Christians, you could be salt and light in most of your community and social life without having to worry about what government rules were coming out of Washington.

Since then, however, the ambit of government has greatly expanded, affecting our economic, personal, and religious liberty. The regulatory state inhibits believers in a number of ways in what they consider the free exercise of their religion. Government itself has taken over areas once considered both private and very often religious: charity, education, and medicine, for instance. These realms once had very important roles for religious faith and are today very much affected by the government, which imposes its own dictates and rules. Today, this expansion of the governmental sphere is creating greater social conflict and resistance to government policy. It's hard to imagine it being otherwise.

A citizen might reluctantly give way before state dictates concerning political or personal preferences. But, if you're a religious believer convinced that God requires a particular course of action, you may very well feel you have little choice but to refuse a similar government demand affecting your religious liberty. No one gains from that kind of confrontation. Thus, in a world with so many changes, we need to think through the theory of religious liberty, how to protect it, and how strong that protection should be.

Controversies involving the relationship between faith and politics go back to humankind's beginnings. Politics and religion were often entwined. Public officials and clerics often attempted to dominate and use one another. There was no stronger buttress for political power than to proclaim that you were responding to God's dictates, whatever god you claimed to be serving. Ancient empires tended to merge the two realms. In the Old Testament world, Judaism had its own state that embodied, sustained, and protected the official faith.

Christianity began as an outcast faith, of course. With the conversion of Emperor Constantine, however, Christianity became the imperial religion and then took on many of the negative attributes that came from that. Even after the empire's collapse, the Roman Catholic Church fought for a very long time to retain a central political role—causing many battles over the years. Today, the Orthodox Church in the East, which arose out of the geographical division of the Roman Empire, pursues many of these same approaches, such as a central political role. We see, for example, a revival of the Orthodox Church and its political role in Russia.

Divisions within Christendom in general undermined support for a united religious political order. Various models competed: Catholic, Lutheran, Reformed and other Protestant sects, Orthodox, and non-Christian faiths. This fracturing on the theological side created leeway for dissenters and ultimately led to political turbulence. In Great Britain, an important model for the United States, the king wished to divorce his queen and thus decided to get rid of the Catholic Church and start his own. I suppose it's nice to have that power—I'm going to create my own church, and we are going to do it my way. Nevertheless, that was a very important part of this battle. We begin to see the political and religious systems pulling apart—including fights between kings, parliaments, and others.

Today, there is much greater separation between the religious and political realms within Christendom. Many countries in Europe have vestigial state churches, but the only question is whether there is a public role for religion at all or it should disappear altogether. However, in some of the Orthodox countries, and certainly in predominantly Islamic nations—in which one sees less separation of church and state—the debate over the role of religion is ongoing.

It is critically important to find some kind of consensus on the role of faith because religion drives human behavior more powerfully than politics. Religion speaks to the transcendent, generating principles regarding both what must be done and what ought to be done. As such, spiritual views usually trump economic, political, and social opinions. Religion is really the ultimate trump. A few years ago, a cartoon in *Christianity Today* showed a room with several people around a table with one person saying, "I see that

Donald, Freda, and George are for the measure, but God and I are against it." That is the extraordinary kind of power that comes from claiming you have the divine on your side.

Expecting people to violate their conscience rather than violate the law is to trust hope rather than experience. This makes the spiritual impulse so very powerful and, for the political order, so very dangerous. If I think that God, the all-powerful creator of the universe, is on my side, then I am on the side of the winner regardless of what happens today. No matter what kind of short-term failures occur, I must stand with him and therefore reject the political order.

Moreover, religion reaches beyond simple belief. There has been some talk recently about the freedom of worship as opposed to freedom of religion, suggesting some degree of internationalization or privatization of faith. For Christianity at least, faith cannot be internalized. It requires action; it motivates conduct. Believers live out their faith with others, as is true in most faiths. Religion takes on most of its power in community. In a favorite parable in the New Testament, the question is about who has been good and who has been bad during life. Jesus asks, have they fed the hungry, have they clothed the naked, have they helped the sick? And he declares, "Whatever you did for the least of these brothers of mine, you did for me." In other words, there is an expectation that you will live out that faith, you will be salt and light. So, one cannot privatize that faith.

That brings us to the current issues facing faith-based businesses. Do people live out their faith in business, as was asked in the *Hobby Lobby* case and many others? Looking at religion as faith, there are a series of concentric rings. First, faith enriches the individual; then those responsibilities radiate outward to family, church, and other intimate forms of community. Ultimately, Christians, in the book of Galatians, are instructed by the apostle Paul to do good to all people. The question of how a Christian lives out this mandate has taken on greater urgency today because of the expanding role of government.

Changes in social attitudes matter, but so does the changing role of a government that is taking in larger swaths of human activity. As I mentioned at the outset, when this nation started, politics controlled a fairly small area of life. Of course, politics was important and hard fought: consider Adams versus Jefferson and the Federalists versus the Anti-Federalists. We complain these days about the incivility in the political process, but those debates were as nasty as anything we see today. Nevertheless, consider, for example, the question of Obamacare, which has affected a whole range of activities. The reason we are arguing about whether the government can mandate that health insurance cover contraception is that the government has taken over an area of life in a more dramatic way than in the past.

In the past, interpretations of the First Amendment and arguments over jurisprudential doctrine were important, but they had more limited applications than what we see today. The scope of government regulation has transformed questions about how we protect religious expression. If religious freedom goes beyond worship—if it is more than a private kind of faith—then the implications are extraordinary in our dramatically different world. The first question is how individuals and families live out their faiths—how one responds to the transcendent. The second question concerns how that affects community, shaping how individuals live, work, and play with each other. After that, we get to questions about broader society.

When people feel confident that the dictates of their faith will be respected, they are more willing to cooperate with other citizens despite disagreements, and they are much less likely to see government and politics as a scorched-earth affair. If you believe that your fundamental liberties are being threatened by the state, then you will likely have a very different attitude toward politics. I have seen this in my own church: some people are very concerned about the future and perceived threats to their faith, and they voice those concerns in ways that worry me.

Managing divergent views of the transcendent is going to be an extraordinary challenge for us in the years ahead.

These issues weren't nearly so complicated in America's early years. It's not that we were a Christian country. People held a wide variety of attitudes, including a number of early leaders who ranged from deists to free thinkers; and we certainly did not create a Christian government. But the world view was widely shared. Thomas Jefferson, despite his deistic views, asked if the liberties of a nation can be secure if we have removed the only firm basis for the conviction that our liberties are gifts of God. These underlying shared beliefs made navigating the issue of religious liberty a bit easier.

America today is totally different. We have a much wider range of spiritual beliefs and attitudes, as well as beliefs about the appropriateness of bringing those convictions into the public realm and political process. In addition, the range of cultural attitudes beyond religion concerning the appropriateness of different behaviors—homosexuality, for example—has widened as well. As a result, the political climate is more charged and difficult.

The First Amendment was an attempt to reduce this kind of conflict within society. The Founders came from Europe, which had spent centuries in religious warfare, centuries using different forms of religious coercion, and centuries of one group fighting for freedom and then imposing its views on others. Americans certainly did not want that in their new world.

The challenge today is similar, and we must search for a balance. We must protect the freedom to respond to the transcendent individually and at the same time not impose that vision on others. And we must do so while the public sphere is constantly expanding. The government doesn't just run the courthouse anymore—it now runs the airport, the hospital, the school, and more. And if it doesn't run something, it funds it. For example, the welfare state includes government-run programs, government funding for private charitable groups, and government-provided volunteers for private charitable groups. Government touches almost everything.

The challenge is to come up with rules that allow us to live our faith while not imposing it on others. We want not only to increase liberty—an extraordinarily important objective—but also to reduce the potential for social conflict over these issues. Society itself benefits if people perceive that the most meaningful aspects of their lives are not being challenged.

The First Amendment does not presume that religion and theological arguments are superior to other judgments, but it does recognize that those who hold religious convictions view themselves as subject to a higher power (i.e., another sovereign). Bringing two sovereigns—government and God—into conflict is likely to create problems not only for the individual but also for the state. Today, it seems that many who don't hold religious beliefs underestimate this potential for conflict.

After all, if one views religion as a form of nonsense, then being forced to listen to a prayer is an irritating waste of time. Forcing people to act against their conscience creates disjunctions that are important to recognize. And if you try to suppress faith, that conflict increases. The resulting problems flow not only to the individual but also to the community and into the political order. When these disputes become part of the political order, we all lose something. We live in a time when a seemingly small dispute— such as whether a wedding venue allows same-sex marriages— suddenly becomes a political issue with legislation and court cases. Today, some people think that you have to give up the external aspects of your faith as a price of citizenship. None of this is healthy for those involved or for the political order.

This was certainly not the vision of the Founders. Whatever their theological views, they recognized that faith is important and its application goes beyond the individual. People of faith need to be allowed to live by conviction in more than just their own home and their place of worship. This challenge is extraordinary because our history warns of the dangers of religious conflict; our history teaches us the importance of maintaining social peace and establishing rules of engagement whereby we can live together in a very diverse society while having radically different visions of the transcendent. If we don't meet this challenge, we may drive one set of citizens toward viewing the political order as illegitimate. And that is in no one's interest.

6. Panel Discussion I

Moderated by Trevor Burrus

Audience Member 1 (Roger Pilon):

Robby, I perked up when I heard you say that the good is prior to the right and even to rights, and I perked up because of the well-known epistemological problem surrounding questions of propositions about the good. There's everyone from David Hume to G. E. Moore to economists who tell us there is no accounting for taste. And given that, in areas such as speech and the First Amendment, we defend the right to be wrong in any number of ways, I am wondering if at least in the political context, it's not the case that the right is superior to the good.

Robert P. George:

The right is prior to the good, I didn't say superior to the good.

Audience Member 1 (Roger Pilon):

Yes, prior to the good.

Robert P. George:

So I am rejecting Rawls's anti-perfectionism: the idea that you can come up with a theory of rights. Now, I do think having a theory of rights is important, so I am not one of those people like Joan Lockwood O'Donovan and some other political theorists that think that the very idea of rights is corrupt, that it is associated with a kind of radical individualism that celebrates selfishness, or anything like that. I think rights are very important, but what I reject is what John Stuart Mill—with whom I disagree on some important things like utilitarianism—rejected when he rejected the idea of basing liberty on the concept of abstract right. Remember, when he says that, he forgoes any advantage to his argument based on appeal to abstract rights. Unfortunately, though, from my point of view, he goes on to say that he considers utility to be the ultimate arbiter in all moral matters. I think you can take his basic insight that rights don't fall down from the heavens. There has to be basis for them. There has to be a grounding in human nature and therefore human good—the well-being of human beings—for them. That doesn't alter in any way their stringency; my only problem with Mill is that he conceives the human good in a utilitarian fashion. And I just don't think that can be sustained, mainly because of the diversity of human goods. There are many aspects of human well-being and fulfillment that give us more than sufficient, more than merely instrumental, reasons for action. They cannot be brought into commensurability with each other so that we can make coherent either Bentham's maxim to do what is for the greatest good for the greatest number (or the more sophisticated contemporary utilitarianism versions of that rule—such as choosing the option in morally significant circumstances of choice that promises to produce the net best proportion of benefit to harm), or if your accepted maxim of harm is hedonic in Bentham's sense, or it is something else. So I need a replacement for utilitarianism, but I think it is critical that we go with Mill on the idea of rejecting abstract rights.

So even a fundamental freedom, like the right to say things that are not true, is rooted in the value for the human being—and relatedly, the value for the community—of honoring freedom of speech. The right itself is an abstract, it doesn't come from nowhere; it comes from something, and that something is the integral well-being of people who we value enough to ascribe rights to—the people who we think have something more than those creatures like amoebae or worms that we do not ascribe rights to.

Audience Member 2:

Think of the two great crises in American history: the Revolution, when many of the Tories followed Paul's exhortation from one of his epistles to "obey God, and honor the king" and could not find any religious reason to take up arms against Great Britain; and the American Civil War, when Lincoln himself in his second inaugural address said that both sides pray to the same god. Aristotle himself said some men are slaves by nature, and this was, I think, the official teaching of the Roman Church. In cases like these, when men and women of good faith take up arms, as they did in the case of the Revolution and the American Civil War, essentially, do you not have to fall back on purely civil law rather than give any objective credence to the religious beliefs of the combatants?

Robert P. George:

I don't understand how you could. And this is for the reasons that Martin Luther King articulated so well in those remarks from the Birmingham jail that I opened my presentation with. There has got to be something underneath the merely human law that enables us to say the law is unjust. Now where does that something come from? King talks about "the natural law," "the eternal law," and "the law of God," quoting St. Augustine and St. Thomas Aquinas. He is not just blowing smoke there. He is sophisticated—he has a Boston University PhD in theology—and he knows this tradition, and it's not just rhetoric. The reason he believes you need a foundation in the natural law or the law of God is because otherwise you have no standard by which to judge the merely human law. Now you might say that at least the human law is more or less objective in the sense that people can read it and know what it says. We have reason to know from our own experience with courts that this is a bit exaggerated, but still there is something to it. Even the purest and ablest men and women have disagreed about fundamental morality, to which my answer—and I assume King's answer—would be "sorry, life's tough." In this veil of tears, we are going to disagree even about fundamental things. And what we must strive to do is to keep our disagreements civil. Learn to be people of conviction who will fight for their convictions, willing to try to win but to try to win victories that we know will never be anything but tentative, subject in a democratic process to being reversed someday for better or for worse and reminding ourselves that, whatever we might think ourselves about a church or a pope's infallibility, we are not infallible, and it could be that we are wrong so we had better be open to argument.

Audience Member 3:

But even so, don't you think that foundation would come from within one's own sense and one's own conscience, and coming to understand what you think at that level is to come to understand who you are? So that it is not going to appeal to anything outside yourself, is always going to then raise the question of what is the foundation for your belief in that, and ultimately, someone has to say, "I believe it because this is what I believe to be true"?

Robert P. George:

Well, that's just a tautology. I believe it because I believe it. What you are probably going to be consulting is what Justice Oliver Wendell Holmes called your viscera. You're going to be consulting your feelings. Actual argument and civil engagement on fundamental issues are tough; I go around the country speaking with Cornell West. It's tough: you have to think hard, you disagree, you hate disagreeing, you wish you could come together on some things. But as hard as that is, as difficult as it is to reach agreed-upon conclusions, it is still better than just essentially saying, "Well, this is how I feel." We need to reason about these things. And we need to reason about these things together. We cannot just look inward. Conscience doesn't work that way. Conscience is not just some faculty independent of reason by which we figure out what is morally true. Conscience is nothing other than one's last best judgment on the basis of faith and reason about what one must do or not do.

If all you're saying is that someone should act on their convictions, then that's true. But then the question is, how should you shape your convictions? How should you inform your conscience? And that requires thinking, arguing, being open to argument, recognizing your own fallibility, developing the virtue of intellectual humility, and at the same time being a person of conviction willing to act.

SECTION II:

RELIGION AND EDUCATION:
THE CONSTANT BATTLEGROUND

7. Religious Liberty in Education

Charles L. Glenn

Twenty years ago, Cato published my report on *Educational Freedom in Eastern Europe*,[1] commissioned by the first Bush administration and then suppressed by the incoming Clinton administration. I had the pleasure of giving copies of that Cato book to education reformers in Ukraine during my recent visits there to advise on how schooling can promote freedom and authentic democracy.

I mention that study because of its two primary themes: the way in which government can misuse popular schooling to seek to impose uniformity and obedience, and the way in which many families, when given a chance, will seek to create or to choose schools for their children reflecting their deepest convictions. My report documented how such initiatives were a primary expression of new freedoms as communist regimes fell; this made it unwelcome to the American education establishment and its allies.

Now, we face a widespread perception that religious liberty is under threat in the United States and, perhaps most critically, in education. Four aspects of religious liberty are essential to this discussion. First, religious liberty protects what is precious to human beings at the most fundamental level. More than identities based on race, ethnicity, gender, or political views, religious convictions "go all the way down," shaping how the believer understands the world and the requirements of a flourishing life, what is worth living for and perhaps worth dying for. A wise polity protects religious liberty, not only to respect the convictions of citizens, but also for the sake of domestic tranquility.

Second, in most cases, meaningful religious liberty is not a private, individualistic affair. With rare exceptions, religious convictions are acquired and supported communally, and expressed in communal acts of worship, fellowship, and service. Religious liberty protects the freedom of voluntary associations to organize and define themselves. The postwar development of international norms for freedom in a variety of spheres of life owes much to the philosophical concept of "personalism" developed by Jacques Maritain and other Catholic and Protestant thinkers, "centered in the dignity of the human person" in relation to other persons.[2] Religious liberty must recognize this social dimension of "human beings . . . not as solitary individuals, but in conjunction with other human beings."[3]

Third, the right to seek to pass on one's religious convictions, especially to one's children, is a fundamental aspect of religious liberty. Jack Coons reminds us, "The right to form families and to determine the scope of their children's practical liberty is for most men and women the primary occasion for choice and responsibility. One does not have to be rich or well placed to experience the family. The opportunity over a span of fifteen or twenty years to attempt the transmission of one's deepest values to a beloved child provides a unique arena for the creative impulse. Here is the communication of ideas in its most elemental mode. Parental expression, for all its invisibility to the media, is an activity with profound First Amendment implications."[4]

And, finally, flourishing religious liberty is a guardian for other freedoms, since "it posits the ultimate limit on the power of the state. The status of religious liberty in a society is a very good empirical measure of the general condition of rights and liberties in that society."[5] This is because, Peter Berger points out, "religion . . . relativizes, puts in their proper place, all the realities of this world, including all institutions." The state "that guarantees religious liberty does more than acknowledge yet another human right: it acknowledges, perhaps without knowing it, that its power is less than ultimate."[6] But perhaps this point was made best by James Madison in 1785, in the *Memorial and Remonstrance*:

> It is the duty of every man to render to the Creator such homage and such only as he believes to be acceptable to him. This duty is precedent, both in order of time and in degree of obligation, to the claims of Civil Society. . . . if a member of Civil Society, who enters into any subordinate Association, must always do it with a reservation of his duty to the General Authority; much more must any man who becomes a member of any particular Civil Society, do it with a saving of his allegiance to the Universal Sovereign. We maintain therefore that in matters of Religion, no man's right is abridged by the institution of Civil Society, and that Religion is wholly exempt from its cognizance.[7]

Much, then, and arguably everything, is at stake in how the religious freedom rights of individuals, of faith-based religious associations, and of parents are protected.

After many years as a state government official and then as an educational policy consultant in many countries, I have become convinced that the *only* way that these rights can be protected in the educational system is through structural pluralism. That requires encouraging a rich variety of schools with distinctive educational missions and allowing parents to choose those that best match their own convictions about education, whether those convictions are based on religious or philosophical beliefs about how children can best be nurtured to maturity.

Americans differ too widely in their faith-based convictions about the nature of a worthy human life and about the possibility of authoritative moral standards to achieve a satisfactory lowest-common-denominator education. As Jonathan Zimmerman has shown in fascinating detail, "no simple compromise could 'solve' the problem of sex education, which touched upon the deepest religious and philosophical rifts in post–World War II America."[8]

But the issue is not simply about how to deal with questions of sexuality, or with enriching the history and social studies curriculum to reflect religious as well as ethnic and gender diversity. The importance of structural pluralism in education is not as a way to avoid such issues, but rather as the only way, in a diverse society, to provide each child with a coherent educational setting based on a shared worldview that the child's parents can support wholeheartedly.

Simply removing offensive elements of the curriculum is not enough to satisfy parents with strong convictions about the education of their children. Because a common school must be minimally acceptable to everyone, it is unlikely to be fully acceptable to anyone with clear views about the best interests of his or her children.

When public schools in the 19th century removed anti-Catholic textbooks, that did not prevent the creation of distinctively Catholic schools. More recently, the prohibition of teacher-led prayer in public schools became a symbolic rallying point for alienation from trends in the wider culture, leading to the explosive growth of Evangelical schooling. Likewise, the absence of anti-Semitic slurs in the curriculum has not prevented the recent rapid growth of various flavors of Jewish schooling.

Many people deplore—and have always deplored—such alternatives, as I showed in *The Myth of the Common School*[9] and more recently in *The American Model of State and School*.[10] They charge that children can learn to be good Americans only through attending public schools, segregated as these are by race and class. Such warnings persist despite massive research evidence to the contrary.

My own research team at Boston University has been interviewing in Islamic high schools across the United States for the past several years. We found that parents and students alike are looking for something they have not found in local public schools. That, not reaction to anti-Muslim hostility, is what draws them to Islamic schools. Youths told us that they appreciate the freedom to have frank discussions on the basis of shared convictions, which they had not found possible in the public schools they previously attended.

I find it plausible that such faith-based schools can provide a better platform for critical engagement with the dominant culture than can a public school, "with its tolerance of almost everything and parallel belief in almost nothing,"[11] swamped by that culture. Sociologist Alan Peshkin's study of a fundamentalist Protestant school seems to bear this out.[12]

To sum up, individual religious freedom is essential, but it needs to be sustained by the freedom of voluntary association, by communities of common purpose with a shared understanding of the nature of a flourishing human life. This is particularly true in education. Schools with a distinctive character can best form the character of their students. The freedom to choose a school for one's child is meaningless if all schools are forced into bland uniformity.

Such bland uniformity—based on what I call "defensive teaching"—is the typical response of American public schools to the objections of parents to any aspect of the curriculum. I am not for a moment suggesting that efforts to present the historical and sociological role of religion fairly and objectively in public schools are unimportant; they are required by intellectual honesty and fairness. But we need to be clear that such curriculum enrichments will not satisfy the demands of those parents—and there are millions of them—who want a school for their children permeated through-and-through by a distinctive worldview, an understanding of the nature and requirements of a flourishing human life.

Oddly enough for a country so fond of invoking freedom, and with an economy based on choice, the United States is a laggard among Western democracies in government support for such choices. In a dozen European countries, and in Canada and Australia, public policies provide public funding for parental choice of faith-based schools in a way that only here and there is beginning to happen in the United States. Respect for religious liberty requires that structural pluralism become the norm in education.

8. Religion, Diversity, and the Failure of Education

Jonathan Zimmerman

I'm a historian, and we're taught not to go to yesterday's news. But it is impossible for me to avoid the elephant in the room: for the first time since the 1880s, when Congress barred Chinese laborers, a presidential candidate proposed excluding an entire group of human beings from the United States. In 1925, of course, we restricted different groups on the basis of race. But we didn't actually bar them.

Among Republican voters in the 2016 primaries, 75 percent endorsed a blanket ban on Muslims coming to the United States. Support for the ban was higher—over 80 percent—among supporters of Donald Trump. But even among people who voted for his opponents, 60 percent wanted to ban Muslims.

I would argue, as an educator, that these statistics reveal a deep failure of education. As a historian, I wonder how people will try to explain all of this in 100 or 200 years. Obviously, they'll talk about 9/11 and the rise of global terrorism, especially within Islamic communities. But they will also point to a failure of education, especially about religion. And they'll note that this time around, the group getting banned was defined by its faith rather than by its race.

Americans are profoundly ignorant about the most basic aspects of formal religion. Why? It partially reflects the way we've constructed our ideal of diversity over the past several decades. Diversity in education—the quest to teach about the range of human differences in America and in the world—simply doesn't include religion. We have Black History Month, we have Women's History Month, and now we have Gay History Month. But there is no Catholic History Month, and there is no Islamic History Month. If there were, you'd hear a lot of objections about threats to the liberty of kids and their families.

If schools used Catholic History Month to engage in group prayer or to try to indoctrinate people into Catholicism, of course that would threaten liberty. And of course I would object to it. But I'd also object if schools used the week to teach everyone how great the Catholics are, which is the typical American pattern. We celebrate people instead of actually teaching about them. And that way, we dodge anything even remotely controversial. Group A is great, and Group B is great, and so it goes, right up to that great Group Z. We're all great! Indeed, our instruction about "diversity" represents its own kind of quasi-religious indoctrination.

Once upon a time, our schools taught just about white men. Thankfully, those days are gone. Anyone who says that we only teach about white men in our public schools just hasn't looked at a textbook recently. Diversity explains why the textbooks are 800 pages long and the middle school kids are getting back problems from hauling them around. If you want to know something about Kazakhi-Americans, there's a sidebar about them in the textbook, describing all the great Kazakhi-American heroes and all the great things they have done.

But the job of the schools is not to celebrate Americans or any group of Americans; it's to teach students about them and to help students make up their own minds. And that's what we haven't done. We diversified the textbook, but its title stayed the same: "Quest for Liberty!" "Rise of the American Nation!" Have you ever noticed that the physics textbook is not called "Triumph of the Atom"?

The theme of the modern textbook is simple: we're awesome. We're a more diverse "we" now, but each component group is also awesome. There's a huge contradiction here: we celebrate America as a land of individual liberty, and then we tell each individual what to think. We don't engage in discussions about the really hard questions, which might call our greatness itself into question.

There are many reasons we don't discuss the really hard questions. Some have to do with the accountability movement, which encourages a kind of rote instruction, especially in poor communities. Some have to do with the way we prepare teachers—many of whom, alas, don't themselves have the kind of knowledge and background to engage in these kinds of questions. Some have to do with courts and the way they have restricted what teachers can say and do.

Again, I'm not suggesting we should start celebrating Catholics or Muslims. I'm taking issue with the entire metaphor of celebration, which shouldn't be the goal of school. The only defensible goal, the only one consistent with individual liberty, is to teach people about our diversity, including our religious diversity, so they can grapple with the tough questions. How much diversity do we want, how much unity? How will we teach people to be citizens if we don't engage them in these questions when they're young?

It's not an easy thing to do. If there's a gay kid in the class, how do you debate same-sex marriage or the religious liberty questions about florists that don't want to service gay weddings? It's possible, but it requires teachers with extraordinary knowledge about diversity, including religious diversity: which faith traditions object to gay marriage, and why do they object? Religious questions are at the root of many of our most profound public issues. Our future citizens will not be able to address those questions in a coherent way unless our schools do. And nothing will change with respect to these issues until citizens of every mind resolve to let our kids make up their own.

9. From Battleground to Common Ground: Religious Liberty in Public Schools

Charles C. Haynes

It is my conviction that getting religion and religious liberty right in public education is essential for the future of the American experiment in democratic freedom.[1] That is why I have worked for nearly 30 years to help local communities move from battleground to common ground on conflicts over the role of religion in schools. On the national level, I have joined with broad coalitions of educational, religious, and civil liberties organizations to develop consensus guidelines on how to address religion in schools under the First Amendment. To date, various coalitions have successfully negotiated 10 such agreements on teaching about religions, religious holidays, the Bible in schools, and other contentious issues.[2]

Of course, a religious consensus in our pluralistic democracy is neither possible nor desirable. But a shared understanding of how to apply First Amendment principles and current law in public schools is not only possible but also essential for ensuring that we can live with our deepest differences. Properly understood, the religious liberty principles of the First Amendment provide the civic framework within which Americans are able to understand one another, negotiate differences, and, where possible, find common ground. By teaching and modeling the rights and responsibilities that flow from the First Amendment, public schools can serve as laboratories for democracy and freedom—places where people of all faiths and none learn to treat one another with fairness and respect.

Unfortunately, our difficult history of getting religion wrong in public education has created widespread confusion and controversy concerning the constitutional role of religion in public schools. When I first began working with schools on these issues in the late 1980s, many schools I visited were largely religion-free zones, where religion was excluded from classrooms in a distorted view of separation of church and state. Other schools, particularly in the South, continued to cling to the vestiges of a bygone era by promoting one religion over others. Both of these approaches to religion in public education—which have characterized schools for much of our history—are unjust and unconstitutional. Nearly 30 years later, however, I find that many public school officials are moving beyond the failed models of our history and working toward getting religion and religious liberty right. As a result, more study about religions and more student religious expression can be found in public schools today than at any time in many decades. Religion is coming into the public schools, mostly through the First Amendment door.

Many factors have contributed to this change, including court decisions, litigation, and advocacy groups on all sides. I will highlight just two developments that have played an especially important role. The first of these developments was the passage of the Equal Access Act in 1984 that has led to the formation of hundreds if not thousands of student-initiated, student-led religious clubs in secondary schools throughout the country. Although the implementation of the Equal Access Act has not been without controversy, even most early critics now agree that it has generally worked to give students appropriate opportunities to express their faith in public schools while simultaneously ensuring that school officials do not take sides in religion.

Second, as mentioned earlier, broad coalitions of religious, civil liberties, and educational organizations have issued a series

of common-ground statements on the constitutional and educational role of religion in public schools. The first agreements in
the late 1980s, "Religion in the Public School Curriculum" and
"Religious Holidays in the Public Schools," were followed over the
next two decades by a series of additional consensus guides. These
included the "Joint Statement of Current Law," "Public Schools
and Religious Communities," "The Bible in Public Schools," and
others. In 2000, the Clinton administration disseminated a packet
containing four of these agreements to every public school in the
country. In 2003, during the George W. Bush administration, the
U.S. Department of Education guidelines were updated and re-
vised to comply with the provision of the No Child Left Behind
Act that directed the department to put out new guidance on constitutionally protected prayer in public schools. Although a few
provisions of that document were and remain controversial, most
of the guidance tracks the earlier agreements.

As a result of the broad consensus articulated in these common-
ground documents and the Department of Education guidance,
educators now have a safe harbor for getting religion right if they
choose to do so. When the guidance is implemented well, public
schools are able to go beyond failed policies and practices that
either imposed religion or banished religion to create a "First
Amendment public school"—a school that neither inculcates nor
inhibits religion, but treats religion and religious conviction with
fairness and respect.

Although areas of disagreement remain, there is now broad
consensus that, under current law, students have the right to
pray alone or in groups as long as such prayers do not disrupt the
school or interfere with the rights of others. Students may share
their faith with classmates, read their scriptures during their free
time, and express their personal religious views in class or as
part of a written assignment or activity as long as the speech is
relevant to the discussion and meets the academic requirements.
Students may distribute religious literature in school, subject to

reasonable time, place, and manner restrictions, and, in secondary schools, may form student religious clubs if the school allows other extracurricular clubs.

There is also agreement that studying *about* religions is not only constitutional; it is also an essential part of a good education. This means that public schools must teach about religion objectively or neutrally—not to indoctrinate students for or against any religion, but to educate them about a variety of religious traditions. Education about religions has come a long way since the first consensus statement in the late 1980s. State social studies standards, for example, are now fairly generous to religion, which is in stark contrast to the virtual silence about religion in the 1980s. As a result, many history textbooks have expanded treatment of religion beyond the bare mention in earlier editions.

Despite these improvements, much of the public school curriculum, beyond modest inclusion in history and literature classes, continues to fall short of serious study of religions. The failure to take religion seriously in the curriculum is hardly neutral or fair under the First Amendment. In my view, genuine neutrality under the Establishment Clause requires exposing students to religious as well as secular ways of understanding the world. A curriculum that largely ignores religion or religious worldviews sends a message to students that religion is irrelevant in the search for truth. But serious treatment of religion in the curriculum will necessitate significant reforms to ensure that teachers have sound academic resources for teaching about religions and receive adequate preparation in religious studies as it relates to the subject they teach.

Although the common ground achieved over the last two decades has made a significant difference in how many public schools address religion, clearly much work remains to be done. Far too many school districts continue to muddle through with outdated policies or no policies at all, leaving them vulnerable to conflicts and litigation. Far too many school officials are afraid to fully implement the consensus I have described, even when they're encouraged to do so by the Department of Education or state policies and legislation. And far too many teachers remain unprepared or unwilling to tackle teaching about religions, whatever the standards or textbooks require.

Common ground on teaching about religions and some of the religious liberty rights of students does not, of course, mean agreement on all religious liberty issues in schools—or on how to implement current law. Culture war battles continue to trigger conflicts and litigation in some communities. Especially contentious are disagreements over how to address sexual orientation and gender identity, Bible electives that fail to meet legal and academic standards, and where to draw the line on student religious expression at school events—and, of course, ongoing fights surrounding the teaching of evolutionary theory.

Without minimizing the remaining areas of disagreement and debate, we should be heartened by the progress made on resolving key issues about the role of religion in public schools. The common ground we have reached creates unprecedented opportunities for public school officials to get religion and religious liberty right—or at least closer to right—in public education.

The single most important first step is for school leaders to engage their community to develop sound policies on the role of religion in their schools—policies that reflect the constitutional safe harbor provided by the national agreements and current law. School districts with sound First Amendment practices and policies are much less likely to experience conflicts and lawsuits over issues related to religion in public schools. Moreover, schools that get religion right build trust and support in their communities.

It will take work. But if American schools and communities seize the opportunity afforded by the First Amendment consensus, a common vision for the common good may yet be realized in public education and in our nation as we undertake the challenging task of forging one nation of many faiths and beliefs in the 21st century.

10. Public Schooling and Religious Equality Cannot Coexist

Neal McCluskey

I wish to make two points: public schooling inherently creates religious conflicts in a pluralistic society, and public schooling is unavoidably discriminatory.

Public schooling has been a historical flash point for a fair number of religious conflicts. Most people tend to think of Catholic and Protestant conflicts, but, in the beginning of public schools, there were conflicts between more or less orthodox Protestants about what schools would teach. We continue to have conflicts among people who think religion has an important or essential role in education and those who think it should have no official place within the public schools for which everyone pays. Today, even with religion removed from any official place in public schooling, religious conflicts abound.

The Cato Institute runs something called the "public schooling battle map." The map currently includes about 1,500 values- and identity-based public-schooling conflicts, and over 250 of those are explicitly and primarily about religion. It is not a comprehensive collection of every values- or identity-based conflict in American education; it's a collection of those that are in the major media and can be found on Google Alerts. There are likely many more that don't get reported.

Although there are 250 predominantly religion-based conflicts, there are all sorts of other conflicts that have a religious component but are not categorized as "religion-based" first and foremost.

Many freedom-of-expression conflicts are connected to religion—for example, questions about what you can wear to school or how you can style your hair if you're Native American and those issues are important to your religion. The teaching of human origins has, for a very long time, been maybe the hottest flash point, but that gets its own category because it has been so consistent and so time-honored. Then there's book "banning"—with the term "banning" in quotation marks because the controversies are not often about saying "you may not access the book," but about whether the school district is going to buy a book, put it in the library, or even more directly put it on a reading list. Most of these conflicts are connected to religious values, so the 250 "pure" religious conflicts are just the tip of the iceberg.

Many of these battles happen not at the district level but at the state level. Now, though, questions about bathroom access and locker room access are a federal issue that affects us all. Nobody is out of the reach of the bombs and the bullets that are fired in these religious and education-connected conflicts. Often, everybody is pulled in, even those who live in a district that isn't having these debates. With regard to bathroom access, some religions say, "Look, modesty and separation between the sexes are important, very important." We've also seen lots of debates over which religions get their holidays off—something that's been hotly discussed in New York City; Montgomery County, Maryland; and Hillsborough County, Florida, among other places. Of course, we've had debates about the origins and the development of life since at least the Scopes Monkey Trial in the 1920s.

Then there's the question of how religion is taught. This is not just about how districts and states handle the teaching of the Bible, which of course is important, and it's not just about Christianity. There have been fights in California and New Mexico over the appropriateness of yoga in schools, with some arguing that yoga has a religious component and therefore it would be government imposing religion on students. About 10 years ago, there was an eruption of discontent from Hindus in California over the treatment of their religion and culture in a state-approved history textbook. Clearly, religion is still an issue in many public schools. These conflicts show that, although public schools are supposed to have a unifying effect, they may actually have a divisive effect.

Going beyond the conflicts, we must realize there is often inherent inequality in public schooling because it tends to be a zero-sum game—if one side gets what they want, the other side has to lose. If one side thinks creationism should be taught and the other does not, one side must lose. If one group thinks the book *Bless Me, Ultima*, which is one of the often-challenged books, should be on the 11th grade curriculum, and another group doesn't, one side has to lose. And if one group thinks religion is inherent to education and the other does not, again, one side has to lose.

Regardless, everybody has to pay for the public schools.

But they're not really "public" schools, they're government schools. When I say "government schools," people accuse me of using a pejorative to take a cheap shot at the public schools. But the accurate descriptor is crucial to understanding that your government is not allowed to discriminate for or against you. I don't use "government schools" to be pejorative; I use it because it's a critical point to understand. The government should not impose religion on anyone, so government schools should not impose religion on anyone. Clearly, that would be establishment of religion. It is also unacceptable to prohibit religion, especially when religion is singled out as something that can't be in the public schools. That's religious inequality under the law. As a result, one system of government schools can't serve all people equally.

The good news is that we can have public funding of education, coupled with freedom for families and educators. This is similar to what Milton Friedman wanted, which was to separate the funding from the provision of the schools. The government can provide the funding but doesn't have to provide the schools. That would allow both public education and freedom.

Vouchers are probably what first come to mind when we think about school choice. But there's a very serious and important objection to vouchers: people can reasonably object to their tax dollars going to a school that teaches X, Y, or Z. Nevertheless, vouchers are better than the current system. There's far less coercion and compulsion if you give choice to all the consumers of education rather than having a winner-takes-all system. Now, if 51 percent, or maybe 45 percent, or maybe a just powerful minority says, "We're going to teach X," then *everyone* has to accept it. That means much less freedom, much more coercion, than if everybody in a pluralistic society was allowed to choose schools that comport with his or her values.

The good news is there are ways to add freedom to the system without running into the legitimate concerns about vouchers: scholarship tax credits or tax credit–funded education savings accounts. With this system, people would have the freedom to donate to a scholarship-granting organization, and—depending on how the law is written—they could donate to the organization of their choice. Do you want to donate to a diocesan school system? Do you want to donate to a system of Montessori schools? That's your choice, and there is far less compulsion in that system than with vouchers.

But what about the "public good"? That is what a lot of people think public schooling is about. When we're trying to shape the next generation, there are two very important public good concerns: (1) Do we want to avoid dangerous teachings, un-American teachings, however that is defined? (2) Do we want to make sure everybody learns civics, about their role as a voter, about the separation of powers in government, and other similar things?

Those questions raise legitimate concerns, but those concerns shouldn't be impediments for more choice. When it comes to dangerous teachings, the likelihood of schools teaching children to kill certain groups or to overthrow the government is exceedingly rare—and such teachings would be problematic at a much deeper level than a schooling question. As for civics education, it's certainly understandable to argue that the next generation of Americans needs to understand American values, understand voting, serve on juries, and similar things. However, research actually suggests that chosen schools are better than traditional public schools at inculcating civic knowledge and attitudes such as volunteering in the community. One possible reason is this: questions about civics—beyond the rhetoric of freedom, equality, and so on—can get very contentious. What is the role of the federal government? What do we mean when we talk about separation of powers? Should the public schools require students to perform community service to graduate? These questions become dicey, and different people with different values have different answers to them. What we might be seeing in civics classes is what has actually been documented in biology classes: public schools tend to gloss over anything that's controversial. They don't want controversy, they don't want conflict, they don't want parents coming to the principal or the school board saying, "I absolutely object to what you did." It's easier not to discuss things that are controversial.

Additionally, public education has become obsessed with test scores—reading and math scores in particular—and things like civics and social studies have been deemphasized. Therefore, chosen schools might be outperforming public schools in civics merely because they teach it. But that is not the main reason. Chosen schools, especially if they're private, bring people together voluntarily rather than forcing a "community" upon them. Voluntary schools can then have a coherent, rigorous set of norms and values that people agree on when they go to that school. "Choice" means schools no longer have to serve the lowest common denominator; firm teachings can exist for everyone.

Another big fear about school choice, maybe the biggest, is that we'll become balkanized. We succeed in life when we speak the same language, when we share norms, when we can do business with people who are different from us. If we don't share an education system, maybe we'll each go off with our own group and we won't interact. Historically, that has not been the case. Self-interest can drive common language, norms, and values. People understand that if they want to succeed in this country, they need to know the norms, the culture, and the language.

Ultimately, our public school system has never and can never treat people of different religions—or nonbelievers—equally. The public school system has produced, or at least exacerbated, repeated conflict. More important, it is fundamentally at odds with American ideals. Only choice, only freedom in education, can bring true equality.

11. Panel Discussion II

*Moderated by Jason Russell**

Jason Russell:

First, I want to ask about this idea of the Blaine amendments, and, if you're unfamiliar, Blaine amendments specify that a state government generally cannot give public funds to religious schools or for religious purposes. There was an attempt to get such an amendment added to the U.S. Constitution, but that narrowly failed. These amendments started as an anti-Catholic idea, and I think we would all agree that discriminating against Catholics in that matter was wrong at the time. But I want to ask, is the principle behind the Blaine amendments justified, because it would be impossible for a state government or the federal government to give equal funds to every single religion. But at the same time, the First Amendment doesn't say you can't give any funds to religion; it just says you can't establish a state religion. So, what are your thoughts on that?

Charles Glenn:

Well, I'm an expert witness in a number of Blaine amendment cases. The argument we made in those cases was this: there is a fundamental liberty right of parents to make decisions, and the Blaine amendments were intended to single out a particular group of parents—Catholic parents—to be unable to make that choice. At that time, in Colorado, New Hampshire, and several other states, government officials were explicitly saying that the public schools were to teach the Protestant religion, were to

---

*Jason Russell is the contributors editor for the *Washington Examiner*.

have daily reading of the Protestant version of the Bible, and all the rest. In other words, the Blaine amendments were a liberty restriction and were in violation of the Fourteenth Amendment's Equal Protection Clause. I think that's very convincing, obviously, or I wouldn't agree to be a witness in these cases.

Jonathan Zimmerman:

I think Charles is right about the history here. The only thing I'd add is this: I would caution us against what my students have learned to call the "fallacy of poisoned origins." If Charles Glenn wants to argue that the Blaine amendments in the 1870s were profoundly anti-Catholic in their motivation, he's absolutely right. But that doesn't necessarily mean that they are today or that they're invalid. So the analogy I often give has to do with the birth control movement. Margaret Sanger—who is the foremother of the birth control movement—made a eugenics argument for birth control. Her famous argument was, "More children from the fit, less from the unfit—that is the chief issue of birth control." This was during the 1920s, when there was enormous fear that white people were committing race suicide because all these other nonwhite people were making lots of babies and whites wanted to prevent them from doing that. That's all true about the origins of birth control, just like the anti-Catholic dimension of the Blaine amendment is true. But it does not invalidate the idea of birth control or public funding of it. What it should force us to do instead is to scrutinize ourselves and our rhetoric to see the degree to which we have maintained or held on to some of these odious dimensions.

Charles Haynes:

I'll just add a word here. I'm not an expert on that history, but I would recommend Steve Green's great book on looking at that history, *The Second Disestablishment*.[1] That period is much more complex than is usually presented. There are other roots of the conviction that state funding for religion violates conscience and there should be a very strict prohibition on it. It's not only the Blaine amendment or the Blaine argument; it's also a complex story. Another point is this: I think the de facto establishment of Protestantism in public schools was, of course, a part of how we were evolving at that time and actually was considered a great achievement—bringing together tremendously diverse Protestants at the time and getting agreement on that. It is a difficult period to just say, "This is the only way to look at it." I think it's not poisoned, but it's history. Today, we would say it's unjust and unconstitutional. We need to think about the challenge of allowing government money to go toward religion and especially the challenge to religion and what that will do to the autonomy of religious conviction and religious institutions. I'm very deeply concerned about that, and I think that's something that in our time we need to think very carefully about.

Charles Glenn:

We might also ask why, in other democracies such as Canada and Australia, the Catholic schools are government-funded. In all the countries of Western Europe, the government funds faith-based schools. Now, I don't think any of those countries are anti-democratic or discriminatory; it's just that they recognize the fundamental right of parents to control the education of their children, a right that is expressed in the various international covenants that shape the way we think about human rights.

Jonathan Zimmerman:

Here's another historical irony—you know we historians love our ironies: you think about the debate and the rhetoric surrounding the term "American exceptionalism." In recent years, you find it more likely for conservatives to be holding onto that term and liberals to be saying, "Look, we're not exceptional and we shouldn't be." For example, look at how Europe has banned the death penalty, and look at their social welfare state. We should be imitating other countries. But on the issues that Charles and I are talking about, it's quite the reverse. It's liberals saying we should be exceptional, we have this absolute separation of church and state that will always bar or should always bar the government from subsidizing religion in any way, we have to be exceptional. And it's often conservatives saying, "No, look at Australia, look at Holland." I think that's a really interesting irony that we have to figure out.

Neal McCluskey:

I think that, for the present day, the real problem again is that Blaine amendments essentially discriminate against religion. You can actually go back and see that Horace Mann said, in effect, "Let's have a sort of Protestantism that everybody can accept." What some people objected to was that this essentially made these Unitarian schools. You're Unitarian, so that works for you, but not for us. You have a schooling system now where you say, look, if you're not religious—if you're atheist, if you're agnostic, if you just don't think religion is important to education—this works for you; but it doesn't work for religious people. And so I think the problem with Blaine amendments now is that they essentially force religious people to be a kind of second-class citizens: you'll pay for these schools that don't work for you but do work for someone else; then, if you want the education that you think is best for your kids, you'll pay again.

Jonathan Zimmerman:

Religious people are themselves divided on this question. Not all religious or devout Americans agree with the statement you just made.

Neal McCluskey:

Well, that's true, but there are religious people who say, "Why should I have to pay twice?" Of course, what we're trying to do is protect even the smallest minorities in this country so that they're not treated as second class. I think that's crucial.

Jason Russell:

One more question from me, and this is just a kind of practical example of how this might work out in a school on its own. Charles Haynes mentioned religious expression in schools and how it is happening more often now than it used to, and the idea of student-led groups. Typically, these groups would be sponsored by a teacher, I imagine.

Charles Haynes:

According to the Equal Access Act, teachers can act as monitors only, in a nonparticipatory manner.

Jason Russell:

OK. Suppose that a teacher was monitoring, for example, a Christian group in a high school. This teacher perhaps promoted the group—not said you have to come, and you certainly can't get extra credit for attending, but invited students to come. In a way, isn't that implicit pressure on students to think that, perhaps, they need to go because then the teacher will like them and it will help their grade? Or perhaps they feel a need to portray Christianity well in a certain class of study or paper to get a good grade on that paper. How does that play out in these guidelines?

Charles Haynes:

It hasn't been a problem because the Equal Access Act, I think, was passed to prevent that kind of problem. Now, it doesn't always work perfectly, but in most schools where I go and work and see the religious clubs, they are student formed and they are student led. Teachers know that they're not supposed to either encourage or discourage participation. I think opening up the conversation for student religious and political clubs has changed the landscape in schools in a lot of ways and has done great things. When I hear some of the arguments about why we should have alternatives, a lot of the things that I hear about the schools today don't sound like the schools I visit or work with. I mean, some of them, maybe; but I work with a lot of schools that are doing tremendous things to teach controversial issues and to engage students. There are the Democracy Prep schools. Generation Global used to be face-to-face—where students are in video conferences with students in India and Pakistan and talking about their faith and their differences. So I don't recognize a lot of the schools I work with in these arguments. I'm not saying I know the majority of schools—this is anecdotal—but I have been working with schools for 25–30 years and a lot of teachers are committed to real diversity. I do think that there is a worldview that's assumed by many public school educators; it's largely unconscious and it's in the curriculum, and I think we need to push back. I think we should teach multiple ways of seeing the world, and we have a lot of work to do, so I'm not saying we're there. But I do think that public education has moved a long way in that direction, at least in my experience, and we should acknowledge that.

Audience Member 1:

I'm with the Center for Pluralism. You've been talking about pluralism and the very simple way to define that is learning to respect the otherness of others and accept the genetic uniqueness of each one of us, so that conflicts can fade and solutions emerge. I would like you guys to define "pluralism."

Charles Glenn:

I think that's a fine definition. I think pluralism goes beyond diversity, at least as I present it. It involves a structural element as well: the right not only to hold different views and so forth but also to express those through organizational life and other structures, including the kinds of public structures that we find necessary in a complex society. So, a pluralistic society like the Netherlands recognizes that you can promote freedom most effectively through allowing different religious and philosophical groups to have their own schools and other kinds of institutions and have them treated on an equal basis.

Charles Haynes:

I would agree with that definition except I would add this—and I'm going to quote my good friend and mentor Os Guinness on this—that we need a vision of chartered pluralism in the United States, which is why all the work that we've done is based in civic principles and ideals. It's based in First Amendment frameworks, and it has been successful because of that. That's where we can have some agreement, despite our differences; it's our charter. Now, within that framework, I think we should recognize our deep differences, and I think we should engage them. I'm trying to work with public schools that do that. We've got to move away from the unity that comes at the expense of the diversity of our early history, and toward a unity in the interest of our diversity. But we still need the unity. And the unity, in my view, is the charter. So, we need a charter across our differences, and I say constitutional principles, ideals, are the charter. Within that, we protect the rights of people to be who they are. We can disagree as to whether public schools can ever achieve that or do that. I'm working for that in public education, but I'm not here to say that it's the only way or that it's going to be completely successful. But I do think that's the vision that will work in the interest of every American.

Neal McCluskey:

It seems to me that "diversity" or "pluralism" means that all people are different in myriad ways—different values, different backgrounds, different desires for their lives. What we need—at least from a government standpoint—is a government that treats us as individuals. I think that the way you get the sort of cohesive, harmonious society has to happen in civil society. It's below the level of government. It's people themselves coming together. There's actually research that talks about how you bridge intergroup difference, and for the most part, you can't be ordered to do it successfully. It can't be engineered, it has to be something you choose to do. I think the good news is we have great historical evidence that people will choose to do it, often out of mutual self-interest. They know that working with people who are different can be beneficial to them both.

Jonathan Zimmerman:

I would just add one thing: I think that the kind of behaviors we're talking about— working across diversity—are not natural. They must be taught. Whenever I give a talk pleading for the kind of controversial issues that Charles Haynes wants in the school, inevitably someone in the audience will say you're just a relativist, which I'm not. The system I'm advocating for is anything but relativistic, because it requires certain shared ideals and principles to work. Nobody comes out of the womb saying, "I'm going to listen to what you say, and even if I don't agree, I won't kill you." Tolerance, respect for difference and diversity, those are learned behaviors; and the reason we need schools, the primary reason, is to teach that.

Audience Member 2:

I'm wondering what you do with sin, because I think, at least in my religious tradition and the religious schools I attended, it was a fundamental thing. I can remember as a child being told that even to go to a church or a ceremony of another religion was sinful. I think the big elephant in the room is that many of the religions hold that certain behaviors and certain beliefs that other religions may hold or that secular people may have or that may even be lawful are sinful. If you're teaching about that religion,

I don't see how you avoid that. And I don't see how you avoid other people in the classroom who may be of a different religion or have different behaviors feeling extremely uncomfortable just being told that what they do sexually, or what they do with their belief systems is not just different, it's sinful, it'll lead them on the road to hell, even though that road is paved with good intentions. What do we do with sin? Nobody has mentioned it, and I think it's fundamental to the whole debate.

Charles Glenn:

I think that's much less common than you might assume. In recent weeks, I've read half a million words of the transcripts my doctoral students did of the interviews with the kids in these Islamic high schools across the country. What I find is an appreciation of differences, the excitement of the field projects, the service projects they're doing with the kids from the local Catholic school, the ways in which they are playing sports against the Evangelical school kids or the public school kids. I think one of the most encouraging things, if you look at the history of the Catholic Church, is the fundamental change that occurred worldwide at Vatican II. It largely grew out of the experience of Catholics in the United States with being able to function in a pluralistic society. John Courtney Murray and others helped make religious freedom and democracy fundamental convictions of the Catholic Church as they never were before. And I'm deeply hopeful that the experience of Muslims in the United States (if the present craziness which is occurring politically can be muzzled) can, in turn, have an impact on Muslim communities in Western Europe and beyond as they see that, in fact, it is possible for people of deep religious conviction to live side by side as citizens, to learn to trust each other, and to work together. Catholics and Protestants learned that in the United States, Jews and Christians learned that in the United States, and I'm deeply hopeful that Muslims and others can also learn that in the United States in ways that will have a worldwide effect.

Charles Haynes:

I just wanted to add that how you teach about religions in public schools is a big topic, but we're not starting from zero here. I mean, we've been doing this a long time. Many world religions teachers I know, whose classrooms I visit in different parts of the country, are doing a very good job of addressing just what you're saying. But they have to set it properly in the beginning of the year. I think all social studies teachers should be setting this up properly with a civic framework whereby the students understand how we're going to talk about differences and parents understand that we're going to deal with differences. I think [it can work] if it's framed properly and it's rooted in a genuine effort to have a dialogue and not a fight. Students have to learn—as Jon said—the skill of civil dialogue and how to address deep differences. The Essentials of Dialogue program that the Tony Blair Faith Foundation is using in many public schools is excellent at this.[2] I think every teacher should be using the Essentials of Dialogue program to set this up. We can't teach about religions without talking about these deep differences in world views. But if we have a classroom of trust and of civility, then it frees the teacher and the students to really dig into issues that are very, very painful and difficult. I've seen this happen over and over again; we can do this. I think we need more of it than we have, but there are many, many successful world religions courses in the United States today doing exactly that.

SECTION III:

PUBLIC ACCOMMODATION:
WHAT ARE THE LIMITS?

12. Can a Surfeit of Statutes "Accommodate" Religious Liberty?

Roger Pilon

America was founded in large part by people fleeing religious persecution,[1] yet today our own government restricts religious liberty in countless ways that a properly read Constitution forbids. We see that especially today in the area of "public accommodations." But that term is ambiguous. As most often used, it refers to businesses that serve the public. But it can also refer to the accommodations that public or governmental programs may or may not make for a variety of human rights and interests, including religious practices.

I'll focus mainly on the first sense, regarding vendors who have been prosecuted recently for declining, on religious grounds, to participate in same-sex marriage ceremonies. But at the end I'll touch on the second sense: first, regarding accommodations for religious organizations otherwise compelled to participate in Obamacare's contraceptive mandate; then, regarding the Obama administration's directive to schools to accommodate transgender students, which implicates the religious liberty and privacy rights of other students and their parents.

Just to be clear, we at Cato have long supported both religious liberty and lesbian, gay, bisexual, and transgender (LGBT) rights, at least insofar as the agendas of the respective parties are consistent with individual liberty under constitutionally limited government. Last year, for example, in *Obergefell v. Hodges*, our amicus brief argued that if government provides benefits to opposite-sex couples, it must do so for same-sex couples as well.[2]

But we draw the line when same-sex couples turn around and demand that government force vendors, against their religious beliefs, to participate in same-sex marriage ceremonies, as happens all too often today. In 2015 in Oregon, for example, a Christian couple who owned a bakery were fined $135,000 and bankrupted after they declined to custom-design a wedding cake for a lesbian couple's wedding.[3]

In Washington State, the state's attorney general and the American Civil Liberties Union (ACLU) sued a florist who declined, on religious grounds, to design custom floral arrangements for a long-time customer's same-sex ceremony.[4] Across the country, in upstate New York, a Christian couple who own a small farm open to the public for seasonal activities were fined $13,000 by the New York State Division of Human Rights for declining to host a same-sex wedding. In addition, they were ordered to implement "antidiscrimination training and procedures" for their staff—reeducation, in effect.[5]

And in Phoenix, in an especially egregious case implicating speech rights and, potentially, religious liberty, two young female artists are suing to overturn a city ordinance that threatens fines of $2,500 and six months in jail for each day a business, including an artistic business, communicates any message publicly that would make someone feel "unwelcome" based on the person's sexual orientation, gender identity, or any one of a number of other characteristics.[6]

I could go on with many other examples, but the picture should be clear. These are small-business owners, vendors who are perfectly willing to serve all customers in their ordinary course of business—and they do. But whether they're bakers, florists, caterers, entertainers, whatever, they're asking simply not to be forced to affirmatively *participate* in an event that implicates their religious beliefs.

How did a country founded largely on religious liberty get to this point? Here's a very brief political and legal history.

Despite having fled religious persecution, we were often less than tolerant once we landed here.[7] But by the time we became independent and then reconstituted ourselves, we were fortunate to have had several religious denominations, no one of which dominated.[8] At the national level, even if not yet at the state level, that required us to separate religion and government.[9] We did that in the Bill of Rights, of course.[10] And over time we applied those rights against the states as well.[11]

But it wasn't simply for practical reasons that we separated church and state. From the outset, we were animated by individual liberty and by the natural rights the common law rested on.[12] Among other things, that law and those natural rights guaranteed freedom of association in our private affairs, including our religious affairs. And freedom of association included the right *not* to associate—in other words, to discriminate—for any reason, good or bad, or no reason at all.[13]

There were limited common-law exceptions, of course. Monopolies—especially arising from government grants—and common carriers had to serve all comers.[14] And if you represented your business as "open to the public," you might be held to that representation, especially if the public had few other options— although the law was uneven on that point. You did not have to serve unruly customers, however, and you could still negotiate over services.[15]

Modern forced association arose with Progressive and New Deal employment and labor laws.[16] But the form at issue in today's public accommodation cases flows mainly from the 1960s civil rights movement.[17] The long-overdue 1964 Civil Rights Act brought an end, finally, to the deplorable state-sanctioned *public* discrimination in the South: Jim Crow.[18] But the act also prohibited *private* discrimination in several domains and on several grounds, both of which have expanded over the years in both federal and state law.[19] However inconsistent with the private right to freedom of association, that extension of anti-discrimination law to the private sector was probably necessary in the context—to break the back of institutionalized racism in the South. It's at the root of the issues before us here, however, because these private vendors, asking only to be let alone to practice their faith, are charged with discrimination.

To complete this brief background, however, I need to mention the Supreme Court's 1990 decision in *Employment Division v. Smith*, where the Court held that a person's religious beliefs do not excuse him from compliance with an otherwise valid law of general application—the Controlled Substances Act, in that case.[20] That led Congress to enact the 1993 Religious Freedom Restoration Act (RFRA), which has since been held to apply only against the federal government.[21] Nevertheless, 21 states have enacted their own RFRAs of various kinds.[22]

At the same time, in the opposite direction, other states have enacted anti-discrimination statutes covering various grounds, including sexual orientation.[23] And to this maze of often conflicting law, we should add that courts may and do invoke the imprecise common-law principles mentioned earlier to decide one way or the other in these public accommodations cases.

The upshot of all of this, as a practical matter, is that in deciding these cases, whether constitutionally, statutorily, or under common law, it is possible that judges will be able to discern and administer a distinction between legitimate discrimination, resting on religious objections to participating in offensive ceremonies, and illegitimate discrimination, resting on the refusal to serve customers in the ordinary courses of business. But that remains to be seen.

Stepping back, however, notice first that RFRA is an effort to restore a *constitutional* right *by statute*.[24] But more telling still, notice the word "restoration" in these RFRA statutes. What have we come to when we have to "restore" religious liberty—our first freedom? Indeed, as RFRA's very title implies, religious liberty is treated today as an "exception," if and when it's granted, to the general power of government to rule.

Yet, if the basic principle in *Smith* is correct—that religious beliefs offer no exception to rules of general applicability (e.g., rules against murder, rape, and robbery)—it follows that the more our rules proliferate beyond what liberty strictly requires, the more our religious liberty will be restricted. Indeed, what better recent example of that than Obamacare? President Barack Obama's oft-repeated mantra, "We're all in this together," captures that connection perfectly.[25]

If we are indeed all in this together, then religious organizations will find themselves constantly importuning government to be "excused" from the offensive mandates government promulgates. They'll have to plead for "accommodations."[26]

Consider the Obama administration's recent transgender directive to schools. The connection between religion and sexual modesty is as old as the Garden of Eden.[27] And the issues are especially acute during adolescence. Yet, in the name of not discriminating against the tiny minority of students who "identify" with a gender different than their biological and genetic gender,[28] the administration has ordered transgender girls to shower with cisgender girls.[29] (For those unfamiliar with these terms, that means boys who identify as girls showering with girls.)

As justification for this arrangement, the ACLU issued a memo baldly asserting that this does not "undermine anyone's privacy" and, further (with original emphasis), that "no one has a legally cognizable privacy interest in *NOT* sharing space with another person of the same sex just because that other person is different from them in certain respects."[30] In that ungainly construction, "same sex" denotes the sex the person "identifies" as; "is different from" denotes genital and genetic differences. Such are the linguistic contortions one must indulge to try to squeeze this agenda under equal protection. In the end, however, it appears that "we're all in this together" extends, literally, even to school locker rooms and showers.

The general point, however, should be clear. How could this state of affairs be otherwise when we've strayed so far in so many ways from principled constitutionalism? The sheer scope of government today at all levels ensures that conflicts over religious liberty will be ubiquitous. And so I conclude that even more than a religious freedom restoration act, we need a freedom restoration act, which of course is what the Constitution was meant to be.

13. The Dangers of Public Accommodation Laws to a Pluralistic Society

Mark L. Rienzi

Americans hold a wide variety of beliefs—different beliefs—on the big issues in life. We disagree about sex, religion, marriage, life, death, and capital punishment. Generally speaking, this is a healthy thing in a pluralistic democracy. It's unhealthy, on the other hand, to empower the government to punish those disagreements and to flatten them out to enforce conformity. As a general matter, the current use of public accommodation laws—in the same-sex marriage context generally but also more broadly—can have that effect: they are often used in attempts to wipe out opinions or viewpoints that some people don't like and don't think other people should be allowed to have.

Broadening our perspective a little bit beyond the cake bakers, the florists, and same-sex weddings is useful. By taking a step back, we can think more broadly about the ways in which thoughtful people on all sides of these big questions draw lines in their lives about what they're willing to stand for, what they're willing to support with their own activities and participation in, and what they're willing to support with their own money. Here is a handful of examples of the broader range of possible conflicts. A couple of years ago, Chipotle—which is near and dear to my heart for many reasons—refused to cater the Boy Scouts' Jamboree in Utah. Why? They had a deep disagreement with the Boy Scouts' then-view on the role of gay scoutmasters. Chipotle essentially said, "We think their view is incompatible with our views about equality and what's good and right in the world, and we can't make the burritos for the Boy Scout Jamboree."

Many regular citizens feel the same way about eating at Chick-fil-A. A few years ago, there was a big controversy about the owner of Chick-fil-A making remarks about gay people and same-sex marriage. A whole lot of people said, "I don't want a penny of my money going to support that. I won't eat his chicken sandwich because I disagree with his beliefs." And a whole lot of other people, by the way, said the exact opposite: "I want to buy a chicken sandwich from that guy because of his beliefs."

We see this in other contexts, too. Pfizer recently announced that it won't be selling some of its drugs to state corrections offices because it doesn't want them used in capital punishment. Pfizer makes and sells the same drugs for lots of other contexts. They're not death penalty drugs; they're barbiturates that calm people down before the government kills them. But Pfizer has a moral belief about this. Pfizer believes it's in the business of healing and says, "We're not going to sell this drug for that use. We do not want to be involved in capital punishment." Pharmacists across the country have taken the same view. A much smaller number of pharmacists take the view that they can't sell emergency contraceptive drugs—drugs they think end a human life, after the moment of conception. The issue most front-and-center, however, involves people who refuse to serve same-sex marriages: the florist who says, "I can't design flowers for that wedding," or the baker who says, "I can't bake a cake," or the calligrapher who says, "I can't design these invitations."

We see similar examples in other circumstances. A cake baker in Colorado refused to bake a cake with a quotation from Leviticus on it saying that homosexuality was wrong. Walmart won't bake confederate cakes. In the *Lexington-Fayette Urban County Human Rights Commission v. Hands On Originals* case, a printer wouldn't make the t-shirts for a gay pride parade. Reasonable people can disagree about the moral stances these people and companies have taken. Obviously, though, they're all engaging in essentially First Amendment conduct. They're all, at some level, exercising their First Amendment rights to speak or to not speak, to associate or to not associate, or to exercise their religion.

My favorite story is about Bruce Springsteen. Bruce Springsteen won't play a concert in North Carolina because he disagrees with the state's rules on who can use which bathrooms. He's taking a moral stance. He has taken this moral stance about which politicians can play his music at their campaign stops. Why? Because he disagrees with certain positions and doesn't want to be associated with them. People on all sides of the political spectrum take a stance—I would suggest to you—all the time.

Therefore, the question is whether we should use public accommodation laws to pick winners and losers and to say that certain actions are off-limits and impermissible. For the most part, the answer is, "No, we should not." It's a bad idea to have the government pick the winners and losers in the fights I described. The government can keep the death penalty legal but should not force unwilling citizens and unwilling businesses to be part of the process. In a free society, we ought to let the unwilling go their own way. The government can kill people some other way if Pfizer doesn't want to help out.

It's bad if our government uses public accommodation laws to mandate that we'll only have burrito makers who agree with one view of marriage. It's bad for the burrito makers—or at least some percentage of them; it's bad for people who are put out of their profession or their career, sometimes in the middle of their lives; and it's also bad for the rest of us. We shouldn't be deprived of the contributions of a diverse society, something that makes America good and strong and special. We're a very diverse country and we benefit from people of all different races, all different religions, all different sexual orientations, all different political views, all different views about everything. For the most part, we ought to look around and say, "That's a good thing," and it's bad if government tries to stamp it out.

It may seem frivolous to worry about this issue in the context of the burrito maker. So let's consider health care, which is one area that really matters. A decade ago, Governor Rod Blagojevich of Illinois said he would require every pharmacist in the state to sell emergency contraception. One pharmacist owned a small pharmacy in Chicago. Chicago, of course, has a million other pharmacies to choose from; you couldn't walk two blocks from this guy's store without tripping over another pharmacy that would happily sell somebody emergency contraception.

The state litigated that case for seven years, going after this one small pharmacist before the government finally had to admit that it had no evidence of a single human being who couldn't get the drug because a pharmacist was exercising his religion. Not a single person. The same thing happened in the state of Washington, which enacted the same rule. After six or seven years of litigation, the state got the same result. But, of course, a lot of people were harmed: some pharmacies had to close because of the rule; some pharmacists actually left the state of Illinois because of the rule.

Or consider the abortion issue. The American College of Obstetricians and Gynecologists (OB-GYNs) estimates that by 2030, we'll have 9,000 fewer OB-GYNs in the country than needed. That's a big number. In light of that, it's pretty bad policy to tell them, "Listen, you're either all in for everything an OB-GYN can do, including partial-birth abortion"—or whatever the most advanced kind of abortion permitted is—"or you're not in at all, and you're not welcome in the profession." As a result, we'll end up with is far less health care for far more people. That is not only not good; it's also wholly unnecessary in most cases.

Yes, when someone is turned down for a service, the harm can be real and painful. Disagreements about big, important things are often painful. Having somebody tell you that your sexual identity or your religious identity is wrong or immoral—so bad, in fact, that they want nothing to do with you—is certainly painful. Avoiding pain seems to be the motivating factor in the growth of public accommodation law. We want to avoid the hurt of being told, "I don't want to be part of your wedding," or "I think your religious beliefs are evil, awful, and wrong."

Yes, those statements are hurtful. As a First Amendment matter, however, the doctrine is very clear: that kind of hurt cannot override people's First Amendment freedoms. It's an old doctrine that has often been upheld by a unanimous Supreme Court—for example, in cases like *Hurley v. Irish-American Gay, Lesbian, & Bisexual Group of Boston*[1] (regarding a gay group that wanted to participate in the St. Patrick's Day Parade in Boston) or, more recently, *Snyder v. Phelps*.[2] What could be more hurtful than showing up at the funeral of a soldier who has just died in Iraq and saying, "People are going to burn in hell, and God hates fags, and God hates America." The Westboro Baptist Church holds up really evil, awful, and mean signs at funerals, which is of course deeply hurtful and painful to people.

Yet, our country has a long tradition—a good tradition—of saying, "Even when the speech is awful, hateful, and hurtful, we need to protect it." We protect it precisely because we don't want the government to be picking the winners and losers, to choose what speech to exclude from the public square and what messages are wrong. The alternative is very bad. It would be bad if you could force the pro-choice printer to print pro-life pictures. It would be bad if you could force the atheist photographer to go take pictures of the Catholic ordination. It would be bad if you could force the gay-rights convention to let the Westboro Baptist Church have a booth. In a free country, you shouldn't do those things. That's not protecting civil liberties; that's government-enforced orthodoxy.

In virtually all of the recent public accommodation cases, there is no parallel to the Jim Crow South. There's no indication of a broad and systemic denial of service—that is, there *is* another willing cake baker, there *is* another willing florist. In one of the florist cases, the actual damages claimed were seven bucks for the cost of gas to go to the next florist. In a diverse and liberal pluralistic society, that is not enough to allow the government to steamroll somebody else's civil rights.

In *Obergefell v. Hodges*,[3] the Supreme Court didn't steamroll over the opinions of those who disagree with same-sex marriage. The Court in *Obergefell* described the belief in the man-and-woman version of marriage as something people hold through good, decent, and honorable religious and philosophical beliefs. The Court didn't say, "This is evil, awful, and wrong, and the government should eradicate it." The problem is not individuals and groups holding that belief; the problem is enshrining that belief in law to make outlaws and outcasts of other people.

Using public accommodation laws to beat down people who have what is now the disfavored view of marriage—to tell them, "You're not welcome in any place, you can't bake a cake, you can't arrange flowers, you can't do any of those things"—is totally contrary to the philosophy of pluralism/tolerance in the *Obergefell* opinion. *Obergefell* says, "Marriage is really, really, really important. And that's why the government can't dictate what a good view of marriage is and what a bad view of marriage is." After that, it's difficult to then say, "And marriage is so important that the government can steamroll the florist or the baker into being part of it."

14. Religious Exemptions from Public Accommodations: What's the Harm?

Louise Melling

For the American Civil Liberties Union (ACLU), the question of whether laws prohibiting discrimination in public accommodations should exempt those who object to complying because of faith is straightforward: the ACLU opposes such exemptions. We come to that stance as an organization committed to religious liberty and to equality. We are guided by the core principle that religious liberty gives us a right to hold and live according to our beliefs, but not to harm others. Yet exemptions from laws barring discrimination in places of public accommodation do just that: they engender harm, by sanctioning the very discrimination the public accommodation laws were designed to prevent.

This chapter strives to give voice to that harm. Even if we don't agree on whether or what exemptions may be appropriate, we need to hear one another. In particular, we need to appreciate the ramifications of our positions. Business owners have spoken eloquently about the harm they experience when faced with complying with a law prohibiting discrimination in a manner that conflicts with their faith; I have learned from them. But exempting these businesses also comes with harm, to those turned away and to the promise of equality. Our debate will be richer if we appreciate and assume responsibility for the consequences of our stances. This chapter looks at the harms relating to a refusal to provide wedding-related services, as those are most prominently debated.[1]

The context for this discourse is important to understanding the harm. The country is engaged in robust, meaningful conversations about recognizing and protecting the equality of lesbian, gay, bisexual, and transgender (LGBT) people. Protections against discrimination on the basis of sexual orientation and gender identity in employment, public accommodations, health care, housing, and education are at last being debated and passed. At the same time, laws ensuring access to contraception have expanded to address a lingering vestige of sex discrimination.

The increase in protections against discrimination has prompted a marked increase in calls to exempt those who object on religious grounds to complying with these new laws. We see that in the debates about laws barring discrimination in public accommodations, such as retail stores, inns, and hospitals; the contraception mandate of the Affordable Care Act; and housing and employment laws, among others. The claims arise with greater frequency precisely because the country is engaged in a period of significant social change.

Similar debates arose in prior decades, when the nation was in the throes of legal and cultural shifts to bar discrimination based on race and gender. We saw claims for exemptions—in education, employment, and public accommodations—at the time of the 1964 Civil Rights Act, when the government stepped in to protect and advance equal rights for black people. Measures to demand equal pay for women also met with resistance in the name of religion.

It's not a surprise that, at a moment of such profound cultural and legal change, we see conflict. Both sides of the dispute have a stake, and there are consequences if the government doesn't act, or if it does act, or depending on how it acts. In the context at hand, for example, if the government takes no action to bar discrimination on the basis of sexual orientation and gender identity, businesses that open their doors to the public can continue to deny services to LGBT people because they are LGBT. Jack Phillips and Barronelle Stutzman can continue to run their bakery and flower businesses according to their beliefs that marriage is for a man and a woman, with all the attendant consequences for same-sex couples. However, if the government bans such discrimination in public accommodations, LGBT people will see the promise of equality, including a right to be served and the recognition that they are worthy of full inclusion in public life. If the government acts to protect the rights of LGBT people, Jack Phillips and Barronelle Stutzman will face the decision of whether to stop making cakes and floral arrangements for weddings or to engage in conduct that runs contrary to their faith.

And if the government enacts a law barring discrimination but provides an exemption for businesses that object on grounds of faith, there will be harm to LGBT customers that runs deep for the person and principle at stake. LGBT people will be turned away because they are LGBT *despite* the state having passed laws to protect them. Indeed, LGBT people are now being turned away from retail stores after finally securing, in the law, the long-awaited promise of equality. In any number of cases, couples have been turned away as a parent watched. No matter what our differences are about the law, we can surely all appreciate the indignity of being rejected, of watching a son or daughter turned away, of having a parent see you humiliated, or of being told, "We don't serve your kind here."

The harm is not only the immediate rejection. It is also the promise of the law lost, the hope for a new status dashed. By sanctioning the ongoing discrimination, exemptions undermine the historically stigmatized group's belief that the community will ever give them a fair shake. The exemptions undermine a fundamental purpose of anti-discrimination laws: to accord recognition and open the door to those traditionally excluded.

The harm runs beyond that one encounter. It carries forward when the couple approaches the next store, wondering how they will be treated, whether they will again be rejected because of who they are. The harm is about discrimination. As the Supreme Court said in *J.E.B. v. Alabama ex rel. T.B.*, when striking down gender-based preemptory challenges in jury selection, discrimination can be an "assertion of . . . inferiority" that "denigrates the dignity of the excluded" and "reinvokes a history of exclusion."[2] And it is about discrimination sanctioned by the government. As the Supreme Court noted in *Obergefell v. Hodges*,

> Many who deem same-sex marriage to be wrong reach that conclusion based on decent and honorable religious or philosophical premises. . . . But when that sincere, personal opposition becomes enacted law and public policy, the necessary consequence is to put the imprimatur of the State itself on an exclusion that soon demeans or stigmatizes those whose own liberty is then denied.[3]

That harm is not remedied by ensuring that the couple can get a cake at another store. The issue, after all, is not the cake, but being turned away because of one's status as an LGBT person. As the Senate Commerce Committee concluded in the context of the public accommodation provisions of the Civil Rights Act:

> The primary purpose is to solve the problem, the deprivation of personal liberty that surely accompanies denials of equal access to public establishments. Discrimination is not simply dollars and cents, hamburgers and movies. It doesn't matter if you can go somewhere else. It is the humiliation, frustration and embarrassment that a person must surely feel when he's told that he is unacceptable as a member of the public.[4]

Nor is the harm avoided by giving notice with, for example, a sign in the window. We need look no further than signs of our past—"No Irish Need Apply," "Whites Only," "No Jews Allowed"—to appreciate that signage may eliminate surprise but does not eliminate harm. It takes but one metaphorical "Heterosexuals Only" sign to make an LGBT person question whether society is in fact committed to remedying discrimination.

In other contexts, our laws have rejected claims for exemptions because lawmakers appreciated these harms. The House version of the Civil Rights Act of 1964, as originally passed, included a provision that wholly exempted religiously affiliated employers from its terms banning race, color, national origin, and sex discrimination in employment. Congress ultimately rejected that exemption.

A South Carolina barbeque franchise resisted compliance with the Civil Rights Act, refusing to serve African Americans on the grounds that the act "contravene[d] the will of God." The court rejected the defense, stating that, while the franchise owner "has a constitutional right to espouse the religious beliefs of his own choosing . . . he does not have the absolute right to exercise and practice such beliefs in utter disregard of the clear constitutional rights of other citizens."[5] Most famously, Bob Jones University and its companion plaintiff Goldsboro Christian Schools invoked religion to resist integration in education. The Supreme Court rejected the claim, reasoning that "the interests asserted by petitioners cannot be accommodated with [the] compelling governmental interest" in "eradicating racial discrimination in education—discrimination that prevailed, with official approval, for the first 165 years of this Nation's constitutional history."[6]

The context of the Civil Rights Act, of course, differs in profound ways from today's struggle for equality for LGBT people. But the history nonetheless bears repeating here, as a reminder that these debates are not new, and that the harm of which the ACLU speaks, to equality and dignity, is a harm that is recognized by our law.

Today's debates, like those in decades past, are about genuine clashes. They are about people who have sincere religious beliefs and people who are striving to be welcomed into society. For the ACLU, the religious liberty claims advanced in these debates will result in harm. That's why the ACLU opposes the claims for exemptions that would permit those with faith-based objections to disobey laws barring discrimination in public accommodations.

At the same time, we will stand up for religious liberty of the prisoner in *Holt v. Hobbs*, seeking to maintain his beard consistent with his faith; the Sikh denied the right to enter the Reserve Officers' Training Corps because of his turban; the employee in *EEOC v. Abercrombie & Fitch* charging discrimination in employment because of her hijab; and the Christian woman seeking to wear religious garb in her driver's license photograph. In these cases, there is no harm.

Religious liberty, like other fundamental rights, has a limit, and that limit comes when others are harmed. Religious liberty does not mean the right to discriminate.

15. Panel Discussion III

Moderated by Ilya Shapiro

Roger Pilon:

The gravamen of Louise's argument rests on this idea of dignitary harm—which is as loose and vague a term as one could possibly come up with. If you look at me the wrong way, I can claim harm. We can get really ridiculous cases, and the idea that you should have an action at law for feeling offended is a prescription for full employment for lawyers, among other things. But as long as you're going to go that route, if you're saying that a rejection when you go into the bakery and ask for a custom-made cake is harmful, so too is the obligation of the baker or the entertainer or the caterer to participate in your same-sex wedding harmful. And I dare say, it's much more harmful to that religious believer than it is to you to be told simply, "No, we'd prefer not to provide you with this service."

But I don't want to rest the issue entirely on weighing the harms, because that gets us into the issue of whose values count for more. The deeper issue is where the presumption lies. And this is exactly what we lost when we decided, in the 1964 Civil Rights Act, to prohibit private discrimination. And again, I think in that context, all things considered, it was absolutely necessary. How long it's going to be necessary is another question. Justice Sandra Day O'Connor spoke of 25 years; she hoped we wouldn't have to be discussing these affirmative-action type cases forever. But in any event, the idea is that once you go down this road, you have flipped the presumptions. Now it's a matter not of justifying why you come together, but justifying why you have a right *not* to associate with the other person.

And I go right back to old contract law and the common-law right of association. Essentially, the presumption is on the side of "not associating"; when people can finally agree on all the terms, then they associate. The common law had this "right to treat," which said essentially that if you had a business and someone walked in, you started negotiating over terms of service and price. If you couldn't reach an agreement, then you left. One of the terms of agreement is whether you shall cater this same-sex wedding, whether you shall open your farm to a wedding by same-sex couples, and so on. So it seems to me that when you reverse the presumptions, you are indeed in this world in which "we're all in this together," and the burden is on you to show why you want to opt out, not the original, common-law approach whereby you associated only if you had agreed on the terms on both sides.

Louise Melling:

We've clearly, as a society, made a choice—starting with the Civil Rights Act and in other ways—to address ongoing discrimination that isn't satisfied in the normal common marketplace you described, where you can choose to be separate and choose to associate. You can still choose to associate, you can still have your views, you can still have your religious views, you can still choose to be opposed to same-sex marriage, to not want to serve. But once you have a business and you've opened your doors to the public, then you're playing by the public rules. And today—you can differ—but today, we live in a society, where in very limited circumstances—in my mind, though I'm sure other people would disagree— we've established a set of rules so as to work to end certain kinds of discrimination against categories of people so as to achieve equality.

Roger Pilon:

Then again, we're right back to an old debate. And it came out in Randy Barnett's new book, *Our Republican Constitution*,[1] whether "We the people" is read as "We the people, collectively," which reduces to majoritarian rule and, oftentimes, majoritarian tyranny, or as "We the people, individually." That's the debate between us.

Mark Rienzi:

Can I raise an old ACLU case that might be a good one for thinking about this, which is the Nazis in Skokie? One of the things the ACLU did, which I think is a wonderful thing, is fight on behalf of the ability of Nazis in the 1960s or 1970s to march through the town of Skokie, Illinois, where a lot of Holocaust survivors lived. I think we would probably all agree the ACLU did the right thing there, and that, in a free society, even if they have hateful, awful, evil views, the Nazis ought to be allowed to march on a public street in a public town—even if it inflicts a lot of dignitary harm on a lot of people who really don't need any more harm piled on their backs.

I think the public accommodation question really comes down to this: Well, what would you do if after the march, the Nazis said, "And I want the Jewish restaurant over there to host my party to celebrate my march"? Or, "After my march, I want the Jewish baker to bake me the cake to celebrate my awesome Nazi march"? To me, in a free society, the answers to both of those questions are clear, which is, "Sure, the Nazis get to march, and we will allow it and live with it because part of being a free society is you really don't want the government able to pick which views are not expressible and which messages are so bad that we're going to squelch them." But I hope the ACLU wouldn't have gone to bat for the Nazis in terms of saying not only do they have the right to march, but they have the right to make sure that the Jewish baker bakes them the celebratory cake or the Jewish hall hosts their party afterwards. To me, that's a pretty clear line. There's a difference between the right to do it in public, and the right to force unwilling private people to be part of it.

Ilya Shapiro:

Louise, why would you, with Gary Johnson, force the Jewish baker to bake the Nazi cake?

Louise Melling:

I would happily defend the right not to bake the cake, because I think this goes back to the difference between message and status, in a certain sense. So we do not think you can force somebody to bake a particular message on the cake, unless it turns out to be that you refuse ever to print, for example, the wedding invitations for people who are LGBT. But there's a difference, often, between the words and a protected status. So you are choosing more of a pure message. First of all, Nazis aren't a protected status in the context of any of the public accommodation laws.

Ilya Shapiro:

In D.C. and other jurisdictions, political views are a protected status.

Mark Rienzi:

A lot of public accommodation laws protect political beliefs and associations.

Ilya Shapiro:

To broaden that question out again, we have a question on Twitter from Sherif Girgis, who is a coauthor with Ryan Anderson and Robbie George of the book *What Is Marriage?*—one of the fundamental and best arguments against gay marriage from a secular perspective.[2] And Sherif asks, "Should we also let dignitary harm trump some free speech claims? If so, can you give an example?"

Louise Melling:

We stand by the rules prohibiting sexual harassment in the context of a workplace, because that would prohibit women from being able to be in the workplace. I don't think anybody would disagree with this on true threats. That's not a dignitary harm, that's a fear of harm to yourself. As to how Cato and others might think about it in terms of speech, we certainly defend the right of people to say that, of course, you shouldn't have to serve somebody. We defend the right of people to stand outside the bakery and protest. We defend the right of people to stand outside the bakery and say hateful things. We defend the right of people to be outside of the marriage hall saying disturbing things. We defend the right of protesters to be outside the abortion clinics saying hateful things to women entering or to doctors who provide services. That, however, is different from whether you can turn somebody away from your business because of who they are.

It's not dissimilar from what we do around race in terms of the kind of speech we sanction. Although we then say, when it comes to a workplace, when it comes to a public accommodation, when it comes to education, when it comes to housing, you can't foreclose people from participating in these institutions when you've opened up your doors to the public. People have to be allowed to be in those places and to engage and otherwise be served in those institutions, even though we can continue a dialogue and a conversation about that in pretty much as charged a manner as possible.

Roger Pilon:

Louise, these people Mark and I are defending are not turning people away from their business. In the Washington state case, for example, this person was a customer for years with this florist. The florist didn't want to go the next step that she saw as actually participating in and—if you will—putting her imprimatur on a same-sex wedding. And that's the—admittedly, sometimes difficult—line to draw. And whether it's judicially administrable is also a second question. But, if it is, that's the line that we're asking to be drawn.

Louise Melling:

I understand that. And I will say then that you could analogize that to Bob Jones University, in the sense that Bob Jones wasn't opposed to admitting, as I recall, students of different races. Bob Jones was opposed to admitting students who advocated interracial dating, for example. The coplaintiff, Goldsboro Christian Schools, was opposed to integration of the school itself. But we still understood that the notion of the right to interracial dating or, fundamentally, in terms of what it means to be equal as LGBT people, is the right to marriage—that once you offer marriage licenses, you can't discriminate. Once you offer to do wedding cakes, then you can't discriminate and create a distinction as to who is and isn't worthy in that particular fashion.

Roger Pilon:

Yes, but the marriage license and the baker are public and private, respectively, and that's a big difference.

Audience Member 1:

I have a question for Ms. Melling. There's been a lot of talk today about cake bakers, and that's an important issue. But it's really not the only issue with regard to religious freedom for institutions, especially religious nonprofit institutions. One such important issue is the right to hire, and this is controversial within most faith communities. But there are people of faith and institutions of faith that support sexual orientation, gender identity, and nondiscrimination laws with religious exemptions, let's just say, for hiring for religious nonprofits. Could you comment on that? There have been Employment Non-Discrimination Act (ENDA) proposals for years. Is there any possibility of, as Doug Laycock said, coming together at all, not with respect to service but with respect to hiring?

Louise Melling:

We advocate that there should be nondiscrimination in hiring with limited exceptions such as the ministerial exception. So, especially within the context of religious charities, they're opening their doors up to the public. These are large institutions. They're often serving people of diverse faiths. They're hospitals. They are one in six hospitals in America. They are broad public institutions. You don't have a right there to discriminate on the basis of gender identity or sexual orientation. At most you have a right under Title VII to hire coreligionists; so the fact that you can hire coreligionists doesn't mean that you can hire only men, for example. The fact that you can hire coreligionists doesn't mean a whole host of things. And the fact that you can hire coreligionists is not a vehicle to discriminate on other grounds, and we think the coreligionist preference is where it can end.

Audience Member 2:

In Oregon, there was a law on the books for 80-plus years that banned religious attire for teachers, and we got that repealed back in 2010. I was glad to see that the Becket Fund supported our effort, but the ACLU was against it, and I was curious to know why the ACLU wouldn't oppose a headscarf ban, because that was the issue at heart. That law—even though it was intended to ban nuns from teaching in public schools—was actually affecting Muslim teachers who wear the headscarf, keeping them from teaching in public schools because their headscarf was interpreted as a religious symbol in public schools. That law still remains in Pennsylvania and, I think, in Nebraska, the two states that have that left.[3] I was very disappointed to see the ACLU against us, because usually they're the big supporters for religious liberties. So if you could comment on that, I'd appreciate it.

Louise Melling:

I will admit that that's an area where I have not worked. So I will say that within the zones of the ACLU's religion work, that is a place where I think there is more debate about what that means for kids if there's somebody wearing religious garb, and whether that influences kids versus whether people think that that is an important exercise of religious liberty.

Mark Rienzi:

And I'll just say from our perspective, religious-garb bans for people teaching in public school are a way to essentially stamp out our religious diversity and make us all look the same. And that is not consistent with the First Amendment and the protection of free exercise of religion. They do things like that in France. In France, last year they sent a high-school girl home because her skirt was too long, saying that she was ostentatiously being Muslim, and that they don't want people to look ostentatiously Muslim in the schools.

Ilya Shapiro:

Does that regulation adjust for when the fashion hemlines go up and down? Is it 20 inches below the fashion standard or something?

Mark Rienzi:

I don't know what "ostentatiously long skirts" mean, but I do think there are two different ways to do religious liberty. One is to stamp out all differences and to say that we are not allowed to be different, we're not allowed to live different ways or look different ways. And the other is to say that, actually, the government really shouldn't be doing that, and if people are good teachers, we ought to take them as they are.

Louise Melling:

Can I clarify that? If it's a general ban, we definitely oppose. If there were a ban of the sort in France, we would oppose that.

But I know there's a debate within the context of public schools, and there may be an answer to that debate which, forgive me, I do not know.

Audience Member 3:

My question is for Louise Melling, and it's actually two questions, but they overlap, so I'm going to ask them together. You make this distinction between speech and conduct, and yet your argument is on dignity. Do you not think that some words can insult people's dignity even worse than other conduct? And if so, how do you reconcile that? And also, why is not the strict scrutiny test a sufficient way to determine whether there is harm justifying state intervention? You wanted to voice the harm that's being done, but it seems to me if there is enough harm done, then you have met the strict scrutiny test. Explain this to me.

Louise Melling:

So, two things. One, in the context in which I was talking, is about public accommodations. Being allowed to enter places and participate in institutions that I'm going to call public—not in a sense that they're government, but in a sense that they've opened their doors—I think is a critical element of equality. And that compromise, that rule, we can adopt—even if you can still be criticized, even if there is still robust debate, even if you can be yelled at going in. Because for institutions like education services and housing, for example, you shouldn't be denied access to things. And I can hear the responses, "But you're not denied access to this. You can go somewhere else."

And so, in the context of how we articulate why we would have that rule, we think about dignity. And yes, of course, your dignity is hurt if you are called names. Of course, your dignity is hurt if you are told that you are a sinner and an abomination, all sorts of things. But that is a tradeoff we make in terms of having a discourse and a conversation, as opposed to being able to participate and being able to access services and enjoy walking in the door, so to speak.

Roger Pilon:

I think the gentleman's question gets us right to the heart of the matter. This idea of dignitary harm is so loose that it allows for virtually any government intrusion. It gets us to the Charlie Hebdo case, does it not? The publication of the cartoons constituted the "dignitary harm." And there are places in Europe, a number of places, where they restrict that kind of speech. And in this country, we just have not gone down that road until recent years. We've allowed for robust discussion and robust behavior—I suppose probably because the proper American response is, if I may be politically incorrect, "man up."

Louise Melling:

You can man up—or woman up today, for one of us. In the context of, if you have been a member of an excluded class, and you have not been able to participate fully in institutions, that is very different. And so again, the laws about anti-discrimination are laws to open up doors. The laws are to ensure that the doors don't close on you in places that we think you should fairly be allowed to walk in. I'm using dignity to articulate one of the ways in which, as we advance in society, as we start to see changes, to explain why it still matters. Why it is not sufficient to say, "Just go to another school. Just go to a different hospital. Just go to a different store. And just go somewhere else, because somebody else will take care of you."

We couldn't say that about the civil rights movement in the context, perhaps, of the South, but people could have said, "Oh well,"—I can't even bear to say this—"you could have moved North." Or, "You didn't have to want to go to Bob Jones University. You didn't have to want to go to the Goldsboro Christian Schools. You didn't have to want to go to those places. You could have just manned up and found services somewhere else." That was not sufficient; we understood what that meant. This is not the same story. I'm not saying this is the same story. But looking at some of the harm, some of the conversations, would you say the same things? Would you ask those same questions in the other context? And if not, why not? And then at least think through what you want to say in today's version of the civil rights struggle.

16. Concluding Essay: Religious Liberty and Religious Judges

Hon. William H. Pryor Jr.

One of the main reasons that many Europeans came to the New World was to escape religious persecution and to exercise their religious faiths. Congregationalists established Plymouth Colony in 1620. Puritans settled in New England to practice their purified version of Anglicanism. William Penn and other Quakers established what would later be known as Pennsylvania. Catholics sought refuge in Maryland. Sometimes the new Americans then engaged in religious discrimination against others, especially against Catholics and Jews. But by the Founding era, Americans had reached a fundamental agreement about the need to protect religious liberty. Of course, the devil remained in the details.

Tocqueville wrote that when he "arriv[ed] in the United States, the religious aspect of the country was the first thing that struck [his] attention; and the longer [he] stayed there, the more . . . [he] perceive[d] the great political consequences resulting from this state of things."[1] He explained that in France, he "had almost always seen the spirit of religion and the spirit of freedom pursuing courses diametrically opposed to each other; but in America [he] found that they were intimately united, and that they reigned in common over the same country."[2] And the Americans he encountered "mainly attributed the peaceful dominion of religion in their country to the separation of Church and State."[3]

Some say that today we are at a crossroads, that the American consensus about religious liberty is changing, perhaps even breaking down. If we hope to reestablish a consensus, we should

139

turn to history for guidance about how to protect religious liberty. American history offers a lesson that the friends of liberty at the Cato Institute can especially appreciate. History teaches that our government and its laws should respect the right of religious people to be let alone.

Throughout our history, Americans have turned to law to protect religious liberty. The Constitution initially prohibited religious tests for public office.[4] The First Amendment later provided that Congress could neither respect an establishment of religion nor prohibit its free exercise.[5] The Supreme Court eventually ruled that the religion clauses of the First Amendment apply to the states under the Fourteenth Amendment.[6] State constitutions provided similar and occasionally even greater protections for religious liberty. And both Congress and state legislatures enacted laws to accommodate religious believers in a variety of circumstances.

Laws, of course, require judges to apply them, and the role of a judge also merits consideration in any discussion about protecting religious liberty. If we respect the right of religious people to be let alone, then we make the task of a judge, whether religious or not, easier. But the converse is not true. If we fail to respect the right of religious people to be let alone, then we threaten to disable some religious judges, in cases about religious liberty, from performing their role in our government.

To examine this matter, I will review two issues. First, I will discuss how our legal tradition of protecting religious liberty has respected the right of religious people to be let alone. Second, I will discuss the role of a religious judge in upholding that tradition and how a different conception of religious liberty affects a religious judge.

Let us turn first to modern history and how the law has protected religious liberty. In 1990, in *Employment Division v. Smith*,[7] the Supreme Court ruled that Oregon could prohibit the sacramental use of peyote without violating the Free Exercise Clause of the First and Fourteenth Amendments.[8] With Justice Antonin Scalia writing for the five-member majority, the *Smith* Court decided that religious believers enjoy no constitutional exemption from valid and neutral laws of general applicability.[9] Justice Sandra Day O'Connor, writing in a concurring opinion, favored "requiring the government to justify any substantial burden on religiously motivated conduct by a compelling state interest and by means narrowly tailored to achieve that interest."[10]

In reaction to the decision in *Smith*, Americans across the political spectrum supported the passage of the Religious Freedom Restoration Act, which adopted a test like Justice O'Connor's rule of strict scrutiny for any governmental burden on religious conduct.[11] Then-Rep. Charles Schumer (D-NY) introduced the legislation in the House, where it had 170 cosponsors and passed by a unanimous voice vote.[12] In the Senate, where the legislation passed by a vote of 97 to 3, senators Orrin Hatch (R-UT) and Edward Kennedy (D-MA) served as lead sponsors.[13] The coalition that supported the legislation included the American Civil Liberties Union, the Christian Legal Society, Americans United for Separation of Church and State, Concerned Women for America, the American Humanist Association, the National Council of Churches, the National Association of Evangelicals, and People for the American Way.[14] Rep. Nancy Pelosi (D-CA) urged her colleagues in the House to support the legislation "because it protects an individual's religious freedom from unnecessary Government interference."[15] She stated, "Religious freedom is one of the founding principles of this Nation."[16] Rep. Jerrold Nadler (D-NY) agreed and said, "If there is a shared American value, it is the commitment to religious liberty."[17] When he signed the legislation, President William Clinton declared its near unanimous support a "miracle."[18]

Although the Supreme Court later nullified applying the act to the states in *City of Boerne v. Flores*[19] in 1997, with Justice Scalia again in the majority and Justice O'Connor this time in dissent,[20] at least

22 states passed their own versions of the act. For example, while I served as state attorney general, the voters of Alabama ratified the Religious Freedom Amendment to the state constitution.[21] And Congress passed, by unanimous consent, and President Clinton signed the Religious Land Use and Institutionalized Persons Act, which imposed a rule of strict scrutiny for burdens of religious liberty by recipients of federal funds.[22] Now, the passage of those laws seems like ancient history.

The political consensus that produced that kind of legislation no longer exists. The American Civil Liberties Union has publically renounced its earlier support for the Religious Freedom Restoration Act. Deputy Legal Director Louise Melling explained, "For more than 15 years, we have been concerned about how the [act] could be used to discriminate against others."[23] Barry Lynn of Americans United for Separation of Church and State has called the act "a sword to harm others."[24] Professor Marty Lederman has described the coalition that supported the act as "fraying at the seams" and "in danger of permanent disintegration."[25] And recent attempts to adopt versions of the act at the state level have encountered stiff resistance and varying success.

There was always less of a consensus about *Smith* in the academy, especially among conservatives, as eminent scholars debated the correctness of that decision as a matter of constitutional law. Immediately after the decision, Michael McConnell argued in the *Harvard Law Review* that "the historical record casts doubt on [*Smith*'s] interpretation of the Free Exercise Clause."[26] But Gerry Bradley rebutted McConnell's reading and argued that "*Smith* rightly jettisoned the conduct exemption because it is manifestly contrary to the plain meaning of the Free Exercise Clause."[27] Philip Hamburger also sided with Justice Scalia's majority opinion in *Smith*. Hamburger acknowledged that, throughout our history, "in various statutes and even state constitutions, Americans expressly granted religious exemptions from some specified civil obligations." But he argued that our country never recognized "a general constitutional right of religious exemption from civil laws."[28] Eugene Volokh agreed with the decision in *Smith*, but he also favored the Religious Freedom Restoration Act as a legislative accommodation.[29]

I do not intend to take sides in the debate about what the Constitution requires or even what kind of legislative accommodation works best. As a federal circuit judge, I am obliged to adhere to the decisions of the Supreme Court interpreting the Constitution and obliged to apply the laws passed by Congress. You won't hear me criticize the late Justice Scalia's decision in *Smith* or the laws passed by Congress afterward. Even Justice Scalia acknowledged in *Smith* that "values that are protected against government interference through enshrinement in the Bill of Rights are not thereby banished from the political process."[30] And reasonable people can disagree about whether a legislative delegation for the judiciary to measure all laws and regulations against a standard of strict scrutiny works better or worse than specific legislative accommodations for particular burdens on religious liberty.

The more pressing question today is what fundamental principle should inform our overarching mix of constitutional protection and legislative accommodation for religious liberty. History offers us a lesson. Our tradition of protecting religious liberty reveals the fundamental principle on which we formed our earlier consensus.

Our legal tradition of protecting religious liberty has respected a right summed up in a phrase familiar to libertarians: the right to be let alone. Louis Brandeis and his law partner, Samuel Warren, first used that phrase in 1890 in their seminal article in the *Harvard Law Review* entitled "The Right to Privacy."[31] That article was about the common law of torts. But 38 years later, in his famous dissenting opinion in *Olmstead v. United States*,[32] Justice Brandeis argued that the Constitution protected that right, too:

> The makers of our Constitution undertook to secure conditions favorable to the pursuit of happiness. They recognized the significance of man's spiritual nature, of

> his feelings, and of his intellect. They knew that only a
> part of the pain, pleasure and satisfactions of life are to be
> found in material things. They sought to protect Ameri-
> cans in their beliefs, their emotions and their sensations.
> They conferred, as against the Government, the right to
> be let alone—the most comprehensive of rights and the
> right most valued by civilized men.[33]

Take note that, even though he was writing about the Fourth and Fifth Amendments, Justice Brandeis mentioned "man's spiritual nature" and his "beliefs," as part of the right to be let alone. He recognized that the right to be let alone informs many areas of law—from the common law of torts to constitutional law. That principle also informs our protection of religious liberty, whether as part of the minimum guarantees of the Constitution or as part of our tradition of legislative accommodation.

Both James Madison and Thomas Jefferson wrote about religious liberty in terms that could be equated with the right to be let alone. In 1785, Madison wrote in the first point of his Memorial and Remonstrance against Religious Assessments that "the Religion then of every man must be left to the conviction and conscience of every man; and it is the right of every man to exercise it as these may dictate."[34] Madison understood religious beliefs as a species of property and wrote that "conscience is the most sacred of all property."[35] Jefferson wrote in "A Bill for Establishing Religious Freedom" that "the opinions of men are not the object of civil government, nor under its jurisdiction."[36]

Our country has provided three kinds of protections for religious liberty that illustrate our tradition of respecting the right of religious people to be let alone. The first concerns religious worship. The second involves the institutional liberty of religious communities. And the third involves not compelling religious people to violate their sacred beliefs when they pose no threat to others.

The Founding generation provided robust protections for religious worship. Section 2 of the Delaware Declaration of Rights in 1776, for example, provided the following protection for worship:

> That all men have a natural and unalienable right to worship Almighty God according to the dictates of their own consciences and understandings; and that no man ought or of right can be compelled to attend any religious worship or maintain any ministry contrary to or against his own free will and consent, and that no authority can or ought to be vested in, or assumed by any power whatever that shall in any case interfere with, or in any manner controul the right of conscience in the free exercise of religious worship.[37]

The Pennsylvania Declaration of Rights in 1776 had nearly identical language about religious worship.[38] The Massachusetts Constitution of 1780 provided,

> And no subject shall be hurt, molested, or restrained, in his person, liberty, or estate, for worshipping GOD in the manner and season most agreeable to the dictates of his own conscience; or for his religious profession or sentiments; provided he doth not disturb the public peace, or obstruct others in their religious worship.[39]

And the Virginia Act for Establishing Religious Freedom in 1786 declared,

> That no man shall be compelled to frequent or support any religious worship, place, or ministry whatsoever, nor shall be enforced, restrained, molested, or burthened in his body or goods, nor shall otherwise suffer on account of his religious opinions or belief; but that all men shall be free to profess, and by argument to maintain, their opinion in matters of religion, and that the same shall in no wise diminish, enlarge, or affect their civil capacities.[40]

The Free Exercise Clause protects religious worship from purposeful discrimination. A few years after the decision in *Smith*, the

Supreme Court decided, in *Church of the Lukumi Babalu Aye v. City of Hialeah*,[41] that the Free Exercise Clause prohibited municipal ordinances regulating the killing of animals where the many exceptions in those ordinances could be understood only as targeting the animal sacrifices of the Santeria religion.[42] Justice Anthony Kennedy wrote for a unanimous Court, "The Free Exercise Clause commits government itself to religious tolerance, and upon even slight suspicion that proposals for state intervention stem from animosity to religion or distrust of its practices, all officials must pause to remember their own high duty to the Constitution and to the rights it secures."[43]

Congress and state legislatures have also provided accommodations for religious worship. During Prohibition, religious communities were allowed to obtain and consume sacramental wine. In *Smith*, Justice Scalia noted that, unlike Oregon, some state laws allow Native Americans to use peyote in religious worship.[44] The federal Controlled Substances Act provides that accommodation, and the Supreme Court has ruled, under the Religious Freedom Restoration Act, that the Controlled Substances Act cannot be enforced against those who use hoasca tea in their religious worship.[45]

The Founders also recognized that religious liberty means that communities of believers enjoy organizational or institutional freedom. In 1783, the Vatican asked Congress to approve a bishop for America, but Congress responded that it had "no authority to permit or refuse" an appointment because "the subject . . . being purely spiritual, it is without the jurisdiction and powers of Congress."[46] In 1806, Secretary of State James Madison informed Bishop John Carroll that the selection of a Catholic bishop for the Louisiana Territory was an "entirely ecclesiastical" matter left to the church alone.[47] And in 1811, President Madison vetoed a bill incorporating the Protestant Episcopal Church in the town of Alexandria, then part of the District of Columbia, as violating the Establishment Clause.[48]

The Supreme Court has upheld, under the First Amendment, the institutional liberty of religious communities throughout our history. In 1872, in *Watson v. Jones*,[49] the Court refused to second-guess the decision of the General Assembly of the Presbyterian Church that resolved a dispute between anti-slavery and pro-slavery factions over who controlled the property of the Walnut Street Presbyterian Church in Louisville, Kentucky.[50] The Court stated that "whenever the questions of discipline, or of faith, or ecclesiastical rule, custom, or law have been decided by the highest of these church judicatories to which the matter has been carried, the legal tribunals must accept such decisions as final, and as binding on them."[51] In 1952, in *Kedroff v. Saint Nicholas Cathedral of the Russian Orthodox Church in North America*,[52] the Court ruled that the right to use the Russian Orthodox Cathedral in New York City was "strictly a matter of ecclesiastical government, the power of the Supreme Church Authority of the Russian Orthodox Church to appoint the ruling hierarch of the archdiocese of North America."[53] And in 1976, in *Serbian Eastern Orthodox Diocese for United States and Canada v. Milivojevich*,[54] the Supreme Court refused to allow a state judiciary to resolve a dispute about the authority of a bishop to control American church property.[55] The Court explained that the First Amendment "permit[s] hierarchical religious organizations to establish their own rules and regulations for internal discipline and government, and to create tribunals for adjudicating disputes over these matters."[56]

More recently, in 2012, the Supreme Court unanimously decided that federal courts cannot decide cases of employment discrimination involving religious ministers. In *Hosanna-Tabor Evangelical Lutheran Church & School v. EEOC*,[57] the Court explained that allowing the government to decide which individuals may minister to the faithful violates both the Establishment Clause and the Free Exercise Clause.[58] The Court ordered the dismissal of a suit filed by a "called teacher" in a Lutheran school and, *in dicta*, stated too that the state cannot compel the ordination of women by the Catholic Church or by an Orthodox Jewish seminary.[59] In distinguishing *Smith*, the Court stated that "*Smith* involved government regulation of only outward physical acts. The present case, in contrast, concerns government interference with an internal church decision that affects the faith and mission of the church itself."[60]

Legislatures too have accorded religious institutions accommodations to exercise their liberty. Churches commonly enjoy an exemption from certain taxes. And religious orders, schools, and hospitals often operate as charitable nonprofits subject to fewer taxes and regulatory burdens.

The Founders also recognized the need to avoid compelling religious people to violate their beliefs. In the Oaths Clause of the Constitution, the Founders required both federal and state officers to bind themselves by "Oath or Affirmation" to the Constitution.[61] The presidential oath also allows an affirmation.[62] The allowance of an affirmation accommodated Quakers, who—on the basis of Matthew 5:33–37—refused to swear any oaths. Before the Founding, most colonies provided that accommodation to Quakers, and in Georgia, Jews were allowed to omit the words "on faith of a Christian" from the naturalization oath in 1740.[63] The federal prohibition of religious tests also accommodated Catholic and Jewish officeholders who would not profess a belief in Protestantism.

Military conscription offers an example of a legislative accommodation that avoids compelling religious people to violate their faiths. The Continental Congress, for example, provided the following accommodation for Quakers and Mennonites who refused, on religious grounds, to bear arms:

> As there are some people, who, from religious principles, cannot bear arms in any case, this Congress intend no violence to their consciences, but earnestly recommend it to them, to contribute liberally in this time of universal calamity, to the relief of their distressed brethren in the

several colonies, and to do all other services to their op-
pressed Country, which they can consistently with their
religious principles.[64]

As Michael McConnell has explained, this policy "recognize[d]
the superior claim of religious 'conscience' over civil obligation,
even at a time of 'universal calamity,' and le[ft] the appropriate
accommodation to the judgment of the religious objectors."[65]

Another common accommodation involves not compelling
clergy to testify about confidential communications. In 1813, in
People v. Philips,[66] a New York court ruled that requiring a Catholic priest to identify a penitent who confessed a crime would have
violated the free exercise guarantee of the state constitution. And
a New York statute in 1828 provided, "No minister of the gospel,
or priest of any denomination whatsoever, shall be allowed to dis-
close any confessions made to him in his professional character,
in the course of discipline enjoined by the rules or practice of such
denomination."[67] Today, court rules of evidence generally recognize a privilege for confidential communications with clergy.

Two major decisions by the Supreme Court in the last century
also accommodated religious believers by not compelling them
to violate their beliefs. Neither decision was based on the religion
clauses of the First Amendment. But both decisions deserve mention as examples of constitutional law protecting the right of religious people to be let alone.

The first decision, *Pierce v. Society of the Sisters of the Holy Names
of Jesus and Mary*,[68] in 1925, recognized the right of parents to educate their children in religious and other private schools.[69] After
Oregon enacted a compulsory education law that required children to attend public schools, two schools—a Catholic primary
school and a military academy for boys—challenged the law as
violating the Fourteenth Amendment.[70] The Supreme Court ruled
that the Oregon law "unreasonably interfere[d] with the liberty
of parents and guardians to direct the upbringing and education

of children under their control."[71] And the Supreme Court recognized that right in terms that could be described as the right to be let alone. The Court described the private schools as "engaged in a kind of undertaking not inherently harmful, but long regarded as useful and meritorious."[72] And the Court found "nothing in the present records to indicate that they have failed to discharge their obligations to patrons, students or the State."[73] Against that record, the Court stated, "The child is not the mere creature of the State; those who nurture him and direct his destiny have the right, coupled with the high duty, to recognize and prepare him for additional obligations."[74]

The second decision, *West Virginia State Board of Education v. Barnette*,[75] in 1943, recognized the right of children of Jehovah's Witnesses to refuse to perform a stiff-arm salute to an American flag and to refuse to recite the Pledge of Allegiance in a public school each day.[76] The Jehovah's Witnesses considered the salute and pledge to be a form of idolatry. School officials expelled the children for refusing to perform the salute and pledge, and state authorities threatened to prosecute their parents for causing the children's delinquency.[77] The Supreme Court, with Justice Robert H. Jackson writing, ruled that the West Virginia law compelling students to perform the salute and to recite the pledge violated their right to free speech.[78] Although the Court declined to base its decision on the religion clauses, Justice Jackson described the principle at stake in terms consistent with the long tradition of protecting religious believers:

> If there is any fixed star in our constitutional constellation, it is that no official, high or petty, can prescribe what shall be orthodox in politics, nationalism, religion, or other matters of opinion or force citizens to confess by word or act their faith therein. If there are any circumstances which permit an exception, they do not now occur to us.[79]

Note his use of the terms "orthodox," "religion," "faith," and "confess." Jackson also described the case in terms consistent with the right to be let alone. He wrote, "The freedom asserted . . . does not bring them into collision with rights asserted by any other individual. . . . Nor is there any question in this case that their behavior is peaceable and orderly. The sole conflict is between authority and rights of the individual."[80] Justice Jackson described the Jehovah's Witnesses as "stand[ing] on a right of self-determination in matters that touch individual opinion and personal attitude."[81]

Justice Hugo Black, joined by Justice William O. Douglas, in a separate concurring opinion, also described the case in terms of accommodating religious believers. He wrote, "The ceremonial, when enforced against conscientious objectors, more likely to defeat than to serve its high purpose, is a handy implement for disguised religious persecution."[82] And he described the religious believers' objection in terms consistent with the right to be let alone:

> We cannot say that a failure, because of religious scruples, to assume a particular physical position and to repeat the words of a patriotic formula creates a grave danger to the nation. Such a statutory exaction is a form of test oath, and the test oath has always been abhorrent in the United States.[83]

Perhaps the most interesting opinion in *Barnette* is the dissenting opinion of Justice Felix Frankfurter, whose views on judicial restraint transition to my final point about religious judges. Justice Frankfurter wrote, in terms that call to mind Justice Scalia's opinion in *Smith*, "it by no means follows that legislative power is wanting whenever a general non-discriminatory civil regulation in fact touches conscientious scruples or religious beliefs of an individual or a group."[84] Justice Frankfurter viewed the Jehovah's

Witnesses as in no position to complain when "this Court denied the right of a state to require its children to attend public schools,"[85] citing *Pierce*. He offered a stirring call to judicial restraint in the following personal terms:

> One who belongs to the most vilified and persecuted minority in history is not likely to be insensible to the freedoms guaranteed by our Constitution. Were my purely personal attitude relevant I should wholeheartedly associate myself with the general libertarian views in the Court's opinion, representing as they do the thought and action of a lifetime. But as judges we are neither Jew nor Gentile, neither Catholic nor agnostic.[86]

I share Justice Frankfurter's perspective about religion and judging. Although religion may properly inform a judge to take his oath seriously, to be truthful and diligent in his work, and to respect the rights of others, religion does not and should not govern a judge's decision about any issue in any case.[87] But that fact does not mean that a judge can ignore his religious faith in his work.

Judge James Buckley once wrote, "A judge, of course, is no more relieved of moral responsibility for his work than anyone else in either private or public life."[88] The *Catechism of the Catholic Church* explains, for example,

> Freedom makes man a moral subject. When he acts deliberately, man is, so to speak, the *father of his acts*. Human acts, that is, acts that are freely chosen in consequence of a judgment of conscience, can be morally evaluated. They are either good or evil.[89]

So what happens when judicial duty and moral duty, as informed by religion, conflict? For a Catholic, like me, the church offers a rich body of teaching that assists a judge in identifying a conflict.[90]

When does the performance of a judicial act become morally unacceptable for a Catholic? The answer is rarely. Ordinarily, the immoral act of a party does not make the judge assigned to his case responsible for that immoral act.

The *Catechism of the Catholic Church* teaches, "The morality of human acts depends on (1) the object chosen; (2) the end in view or the intention; [and] (3) the circumstances of the action."[91] "A *morally good* act requires the goodness of the object, of the end, and of the circumstances together. An evil end corrupts the action, even if the object is good in itself (such as praying and fasting 'in order to be seen by men')."[92] Conversely, "a good intention . . . does not make behavior that is intrinsically disordered . . . good or just. The end does not justify the means."[93]

For a Catholic, there are two kinds of cooperation with evil that must be avoided. The first is called formal cooperation, which occurs when the cooperator shares the evil intent of the actor.[94] Formal cooperation with evil is always morally wrong,[95] but it is an unlikely problem for a judge who must apply the law impartially—that is, without adopting, as the judge's own end, the object sought by a party who seeks relief from a court.

The other and, for a judge, more likely kind of cooperation with evil is called material cooperation. Material cooperation occurs when the cooperator assists the actor by performing an act that is not necessarily evil.[96] Whether material cooperation is morally acceptable depends on whether there is a sound reason for the cooperation (such as avoiding a worse harm), whether the cooperation is remote or proximate, and whether the cooperator avoids the danger of scandal.[97] The graver the evil, then the more serious the reason for cooperation must be to be justifiable.

Two of these conditions for material cooperation are ordinarily satisfied in the performance of judicial work. A judge has more than a good reason to apply the law impartially in every case because the performance of that duty in a constitutional republic is a fundamental safeguard for the protection of human liberty. The resources of the judiciary are also scarce, so a judge is ordinarily obliged to perform his share of the work of the judiciary. The performance of the judicial function is likely to be remote from the intended evil act of a party before the court; in the typical scenario, the judge determines that the law does not empower the government to interfere with an individual's freedom to commit an immoral act. And when the government threatens an individual's religious liberty, laws that respect an individual's right to be let alone empower a judge to shield an individual from unjust injury.

A judge must be attentive to the third condition for acceptable material cooperation: avoiding the problem of scandal. "Scandal is an attitude or behavior which leads another to do evil."[98] The *Catechism* explains, "Anyone who uses the power at his disposal in such a way that it leads others to do wrong becomes guilty of scandal and responsible for the evil that he has directly or indirectly encouraged."[99] The *Catechism* also states, "Scandal can be provoked by laws or institutions, by fashion or opinion."[100] For judges and lawyers, there is a special danger of scandal, because "scandal is grave when given by those who by nature or office are obliged to teach and educate others."[101]

Some circumstances of material cooperation raise serious issues of proximity and potential scandal. A Catholic trial judge in a state court who must decide whether to sentence a murderer to death or to grant permission for a minor to have an abortion would have to consider whether he or she is proximately cooperating with an evil act and avoiding scandal, but a Catholic federal judge is far less likely to face this kind of proximity or potential scandal. Catholic legal scholars have concluded, for example, that a federal appellate judge does not either proximately cooperate with a potential evil or cause scandal when he upholds a death sentence: "To affirm a sentence is not to approve it, but to say that the trial court did its job."[102] Justice Scalia, in a lecture at the Dominican House of Studies in the District of Columbia a month before he passed away, made the same point about a case where the law does not empower a judge to interfere with a woman's choice to have an abortion.[103]

The more likely scenario for a federal judge is that his cooperation with another's evil act will be remote, dictated by law, and
faithful to a duty that more often protects our freedom in a noble
and necessary manner. Allow me an example outside the judicial
realm: a Catholic mail carrier rightly respects the rules of privacy
and prompt delivery for get-well cards, boxes of Holy Bibles, and
life-saving medications, while following the same rules for deliv-
ering pornography. A judge similarly applies the law impartially
in a variety of cases where the law protects the poor, victims of
wrongdoing, the integrity of the family, and religious freedom,
and the judge respects the law when it does not empower him to
prevent a third party from committing an immoral act.

This framework breaks down when we no longer view religious
liberty as a matter of the right to be let alone. Think about some
easy examples. A Catholic trial judge would consider it immoral
to punish a Catholic priest for refusing to divulge a penitent's
sacramental confession. And if our country were to reinstate the
prohibition of alcohol without the earlier accommodations for religious people, a Catholic trial judge would consider it immoral
to sentence a priest for celebrating Mass with wine. These examples would probably create a moral dilemma for many religious
judges. I suspect that religious judges of many faiths, for example,
would be uncomfortable punishing a Catholic priest for refusing
to divulge a confession or punishing a Quaker for refusing to
bear arms for his country. A religious judge would also likely feel
obliged to respect the right of a family to educate their children
in a religious school. Now consider a contemporary problem:
whether a Catholic or a Southern Baptist judge would be com-
fortable punishing an employer—for example, an order of nuns
or a seminary—for refusing to pay for an employee's abortion or
sterilization.

Our country must grapple with the fact that many Americans
no longer view religious liberty the same way. Ilya Shapiro explained this point after the *Hobby Lobby* decision. He wrote that

"an exception from . . . a mandate is hardly coercive, and . . . an exemption would harm third parties *only if* we think those third parties have a right to force others to pay for their goods or services."[104] He explained that "Americans have become so accustomed to government power as the norm—providing all manner of goods and benefits—that resisting state action has begun to look anomalous."[105] Or as Megan McArdle put it for *Bloomberg View*:

> The long compromise worked out between the state and religious groups—do what you want within very broad limits, but don't expect the state to promote it—is breaking down in the face of a shift in the way we view rights and the role of the government in public life.[106]

I would put it this way: many Americans have forgotten our long tradition of respecting the right of religious people to be let alone.

Shapiro and McArdle have identified only half the problem. If we cast aside the right of religious people to be let alone and replace that right with a new conception of freedom, then we will do more than create new problems for religious private citizens. We will also create unprecedented problems for religious judges.

Our country is more likely to regain a consensus in favor of protecting religious liberty by adhering to its traditional understanding of freedom and not by reimagining it. That is, Americans can reach a consensus by sharing James Madison's view that "conscience is the most sacred of all property"[107] and Thomas Jefferson's view "that the opinions of men are not the object of civil government, nor under its jurisdiction."[108] We should do so by reaffirming that religious people enjoy what Justice Brandeis called "the most comprehensive of rights and the right most valued by civilized men"[109]—the right to be let alone.

17. Final Thoughts

Ilya Shapiro

I can't do justice here to the deep and important discussions that resonate throughout this book, ranging from first principles and the history of religious toleration, to the special relationship between religion and education, to the role that the courts play in adjudicating the cultural flash points that increasingly bring religious believers into conflict with the secular world. What I want to focus on instead is how modern battles over religion in the public square are a microcosm of the constant tension between civil society and an overweening regulatory state.

Take the contraceptive-mandate cases, *Burwell v. Hobby Lobby* (2014, regarding for-profit companies) and *Zubik v. Burwell* (2016, regarding religious nonprofits).[1] These cases had all the makings of Supreme Court blockbusters: birth control and sexual liberation, religious freedom, corporate rights, the power of employers, and the rights of workers. The government claimed that this was about ensuring that all women had access to contraception. Many in the media (and several senators), purporting to be concerned about women's rights, claimed that the issue was whether employees would have access to birth control despite their employers' religious objections.

Those on the other side argued that the case concerned every American's right to freely exercise religion. David and Barbara Green, who own the Hobby Lobby chain of arts-and-crafts stores, had long provided health care benefits to their employees (they believed it was their Christian duty), but they had not paid for abortions. The Affordable Care Act (actually a regulation interpreting that law's instruction to cover "preventive care") required them to pay for their employees' contraceptives—including those that can prevent the implantation of fertilized eggs, which the Greens consider to be an abortifacient and therefore against their religious beliefs. Nonprofits like the Little Sisters of the Poor had different objections, but nobody disputed that they were religious organizations to begin with.

These cases, however, were not ultimately about the freedom to use legal contraceptives or the power of big business—or even about how to balance religious liberty against other constitutional considerations. *Hobby Lobby* involved a fairly straightforward question of statutory interpretation regarding whether the government was justified in this particular case in overriding certain religious objections. *Zubik* asked whether the government was doing all it could to accommodate religious organizations, as the law required. The Supreme Court evaluated these questions and ruled that (1) closely held corporations can't be forced to pay for every kind of contraceptive for their employees if doing so would violate their religious beliefs, and (2) a better accommodation could be forged. In both cases, under the Religious Freedom Restoration Act of 1993, the government failed to show that it had no less burdensome means of accomplishing its stated goal (providing female workers with "no-cost access to contraception").

There was no constitutional decision, no expansion of corporate rights, and no weighing of religion versus the right to access birth control. Nobody was denied access to contraceptives, and there is now more freedom for all Americans to live their lives as they wish, in accordance with their beliefs, without being forced to check their conscience at the office door.

Justice Ruth Bader Ginsburg's dissent in *Hobby Lobby*, however, paints a different picture. According to her, by refusing to pay for certain kinds of contraceptives, employers were imposing their religious beliefs on their employees. This understanding was the basis of the "Not My Boss's Business Act" that Senate Democrats proposed to overturn the ruling.

Thus, as Megan McArdle noted at *Bloomberg View* after the *Hobby Lobby* ruling, these cases present the unusual situation in which both sides think that someone else's views are being imposed on them.[2] Normally in political disputes, the debate is over the economic or moral justifications for a particular policy, or whether the regulatory benefits outweigh the economic costs. But in the discussion of Obamacare's contraceptive mandate, one side says that not paying for contraceptives is equivalent to the imposition of religious beliefs, while the other says that the coercion lies in being forced to buy something it doesn't want to buy.

While we can argue about whether requiring people to buy certain goods or services is a good idea, Obamacare clearly forces employers to buy them. An exemption from such a mandate is hardly coercive, and such an exemption would harm third parties *only if* we think those third parties have a right to force others to pay for their goods or services.

That "if" is the crux of the matter—and not just as it relates to Obamacare, gender equality, or the particularities of any case. Americans have become so used to government providing all manner of goods and benefits that resisting state action has begun to look anomalous. The right to freely exercise religion, among many other individual liberties, is thus an exception to the general rule of government power.

The left's outcry over religious free-exercise cases is evidence of a more insidious process whereby the government foments social conflict as it expands its control into areas of life that we used to consider public yet not governmental. This conflict is exceptionally fierce because, as McArdle put it, "the long compromise worked out between state and religious groups—do what you want within very broad limits, but don't expect the state to promote it—is breaking down in the face of a shift in the way we view rights and the role of government in public life."[3]

Indeed, it is government's relationship to public life that is changing—in places that are beyond the intimacies of the home

but are still far removed from the state, such as churches, charities, social clubs, small businesses, and even "public" corporations that are nevertheless part of the private sector. Under the
influence of the Obama administration, the left wove government
through these private institutions, using them to engineer American life according to its vision. The key to this far-reaching agenda
is the conceit that it is the government that grants rights.

Through an ever-growing list of mandates, rules, and "rights,"
the government is regulating away the "little platoons" of our
civil society. Civil society, so important to America's character, is
being smothered by the ever-growing administrative state that,
in the name of fairness and equality, takes away rights in order to
standardize American life from cradle to grave.

This dynamic is just the latest example of the difficulties inherent in turning health care (and our economy more broadly) over
to the government. It also represents a larger, more destructive
trend, enabled by the Supreme Court's ratification of expansive
federal power—for instance, reading the General Welfare Clause
as a grant rather than as a restriction of authority and applying
the Interstate Commerce Clause to intrastate non-commerce. The
assumption underlying these expansions is roughly what former
Democratic representative Barney Frank told the 2012 Democratic
National Convention: "government is simply the name we give to
the things we choose to do together."

One of the major problems here, as my colleague Roger Pilon
has written, is that when something is socialized or treated as
a public utility, we are forced to fight for every "carve-out" of
freedom from its rules. So the more we "choose to do together"
through the coercive hand of the state, the less we can do in our
private capacities, together or separately.

***

Historically, these efforts to carve out exceptions have been
relatively direct and obvious, a function of conventional political
arguments over taxing, spending, and the role of government:

the money we pay in taxes can't go to consumer goods or political advocacy or anything else we may value. Notably, it also can't go toward nongovernmental education or health care, so government programs in those areas enjoy a tremendous advantage over their would-be private competitors.

The government has recently moved past this conventional means of crowding out civil society, changing and narrowing the rules of the game such that private institutions are allowed to continue operating only as long as they follow a prescribed list of behaviors and mores. Obamacare is the apotheosis of this trend: it relies on conventional, government-expanding transfer payments, of course. But the heart of the legislation is a tangled web of "shalls" and "shall nots" that reshapes the health care industry—and thus about a fifth of the economy.

Critics of the health care law have framed the *Hobby Lobby* case as involving an attack on religious liberty, and while that is certainly correct with regard to the cases that reached the Supreme Court, the dispute is indicative of a much larger problem. The Obama administration could have made all the lawsuits go away if it had simply decided to use one of the alternatives identified in Justice Samuel Alito's majority opinion. For example, the government could pay for the disputed contraceptives itself, or provide tax credits, or, for those who wouldn't object to signing a form, make the kind of accommodation it offered certain nonprofits. There are many other possibilities, including imposing the mandate on *insurers*, not employers.

The Justice Department chose instead to pursue a scorched-earth strategy, which indicates that providing no-cost contraceptives was not the administration's main motivation. Instead, the goal seems to have been to force religious employers to conform to the "we're all in it together" ethos. The administration's decision not to compromise in any way is a shot across the bow of anyone who might deviate from this understanding of the government's role in society.

Although progressives may cheer such coercion in this situation, they fail to appreciate the precedent it sets. Indeed, the more the federal government ventures onto the cultural battlefield, the more both liberals and conservatives will issue mandates and regulations toward ideological ends. Through this kind of excessive regulation, then, the government crowds out individual conscience and the voluntary institutions of civil society by conditioning participation in essential economic activity on the relinquishment of certain other rights.

And the bigger government grows as a whole, the more the regulatory apparatus flexes its muscle. At the same time, political appointees and bureaucrats prefer this method of power dealing: they gain prestige and influence handing out favors, increasing their power without consideration for the "off-balance-sheet" costs to society.

The growing enforcement of centralized ideological conformity is a real innovation in the use of government power. The issue isn't that Congress is taxing and spending and borrowing more than it ever has, but that it's forcing more mandates into what used to be private decisionmaking. It is shifting the boundary between the private and public spheres, trampling individual agency, and narrowing the choices that people are allowed to make in pursuit of their particular version of the good life.

Whole swaths of life—from education and health care to commercial enterprises and eleemosynary concerns—are now overseen by those who operate the levers of power. In other words, as the scope of government regulation increases, decisions that were once left to families and managers are now used as collateral in the political deal-making process. And powerful interests take advantage of an uncoordinated general public.

The Religious Freedom Restoration Act (RFRA), which was central to the contraceptive-mandate cases, is a perfect example of how we now have to beg government for our rights. Because the government can do just about anything, religious individuals and institutions had to secure an exemption to do what they should have been free to do anyway.

To make matters worse, Justice Antonin Scalia, a devout Catholic, laid the foundation for this particular problem. "We have never held that an individual's religious beliefs excuse him from compliance with an otherwise valid law prohibiting conduct that the State is free to regulate," he wrote in 1990 in *Employment Division v. Smith*, the case that led to RFRA. Justice Scalia was right there. But, for decades, the Supreme Court neglected to draw a proper constitutional distinction between what the government can and can't regulate. That distinction is at the heart of the contraceptive-mandate litigation.

The Catholic bishops' complaint about the government's enforcement of Obamacare was right as far as it went: "[The contraceptive mandate] continues to involve needless government intrusion in the internal governance of religious institutions and to threaten government coercion of religious people and groups to violate their most deeply held convictions." But pleading for special exemptions did not get them very far, as they had supported the main goal of the legislation. It was the effort to socialize American health care that was the basic problem, not one small part of the bill's regulatory apparatus. And having supported the larger goal, the bishops should not be surprised that religious freedom was crushed along with many other liberties.

Looking beyond Obamacare's restrictions on liberty, we see the same thing in the spillover from the gay-marriage debates, with people being fined for not working at same-sex commitment ceremonies—the Oregon baker, the New Mexico photographer, and the Washington florist. There is a clear difference between arguing that the government has to treat everyone equally—the actual legal dispute regarding state marriage licenses—and forcing private individuals and businesses to endorse and support practices with which they disagree. It is disappointing but not surprising that Elane Photography lost its case, despite New Mexico's own state-level RFRA, and that the Supreme Court denied review of that state's high-court ruling. Despite gay-rights activists' comparing their struggle to the civil rights movement, New Mexico is not like the Jim Crow South, where state-enforced segregation meant that black travelers had nowhere to eat or stay.

As long as those in power demand that people adopt politically correct beliefs or cease to engage in the public sphere, these issues will continue to arise. Marriage itself is an area where government regulation has created needless social clashes: Without state licensure, individuals could assign whatever contract and property right to whomever they liked, have whatever civic or religious organization consecrate their union (if they wished), and let the common law take care of the rest. Education is another good example: The curricular battles over evolution and creationism, or the amount of time devoted to arts versus sciences, or debates over methods of discipline or extracurricular offerings could all be defused if the government allowed parents more choice over how to educate their children. Many of our culture wars are a direct result of government trying to force one-size-fits-all public policy solutions onto a diverse nation.

While the debate over the contraceptive mandate centered on a statutory safety valve that prevents capricious impingements on religious freedom, the larger matter of government's rending of the social fabric remains. Justice Ginsburg, in her *Hobby Lobby* dissent, expressed serious doubts about the idea of exemptions from government regulation:

> Would the exemption the Court holds RFRA demands for employers with religiously grounded objections to the use of certain contraceptives extend to employers with religiously grounded objections to blood transfusions (Jehovah's Witnesses); antidepressants (Scientologists); medications derived from pigs, including anesthesia, intravenous fluids, and pills coated with gelatin (certain Muslims, Jews, and Hindus); and vaccinations (Christian Scientists, among others)?[4]

Instead of concluding from this list of hypothetical situations that *nobody* should get exemptions from government mandates, the more obvious solution would be to allow everyone to have the same freedom to choose how to live his or her own life.

The solution to this problem of special treatment is not for government to deny exemptions to all such that all are equally coerced. Instead, the approach consistent with the American principle that the state exists to secure and preserve liberty is for government to recognize the right of *all individuals* to act according to their conscience. That includes, among many other things, the right to run their businesses—including contracting with others (or not)—as they see fit. It means being able to decide whether and how much to pay for their employees' health care and to make those decisions for any reason, religious or secular, or no reason at all.

Hobby Lobby was one case in which the Supreme Court stood up for individual rights—but only under an unusual statutory exemption, and just barely. The left's reaction to that ruling shows how little they understand, as presidents Gerald Ford and Ronald Reagan said, that a government big enough to give you everything you want is powerful enough to take away everything you have. Or, as James Madison wrote in "Federalist 51," "you must first enable the government to control the governed; and in the next place oblige it to control itself." That is exactly what the Constitution's enumeration of powers was designed to do—limit power. That principle is simply no longer being enforced.

The most basic principle of a free society is that government cannot force people to do things that violate their conscience. Americans understand this point intuitively. Some may argue that in the contraceptive-mandate cases there was a conflict between religious freedom and reproductive freedom, so the government had to step in as referee—and that women's health is more important than religious preferences. But that's a false choice, as President Barack Obama liked to say. Without the contraceptive mandate, women are still free to obtain contraceptives, abortions, and anything else that isn't illegal. They just can't force their employer to pay the bill.

The problem that *Hobby Lobby* and *Zubik* exposed isn't that the rights of employers are privileged over those of employees. It's that no branch of our federal government recognizes *everyone's* right to live his life as he wishes in all spheres. Instead, we are all compelled to conform to the collectivist morality that those in charge of government have decided is right.

Americans largely agree—at least within reasonable margins—that certain things are collective needs and their provision falls under the purview of the federal government, such as national defense, basic infrastructure, clean air and water, and a few other such "public goods." But most social programs, many economic regulations, and so much else that government now promulgates are subjects of bitter disagreements precisely because these things implicate individual freedoms. And we feel it acutely, as Americans, when our liberties have been attacked.

The trouble is that, when government grants us freedoms instead of protecting them, the question of exactly what those freedoms are becomes much less clear, and every liberty we thought we had is up for discussion—and regulation. Those who supported the religious believers in the contraceptive-mandate cases were rightly concerned that people are being forced to do what their deepest values prohibit. But that's all part of this new, collectivized territory.

Notes

Chapter 1

[1] Richard E. Rubenstein, *When Jesus Became God: The Struggle to Define Christianity during the Last Days of Rome* (New York: Houghton Mifflin, 1999), p. 1.

[2] Christopher Haas, "The Alexandrian Riots of 356 and George of Cappadocia," *Greek, Roman, and Byzantine Studies* 32, no. 3 (Autumn 1991): 291.

[3] Ibid., p. 291.

[4] Ibid., p. 295.

[5] Ibid., pp. 288, 292–93.

[6] Rubenstein, *When Jesus Became God*, p. 3.

[7] Perez Zagorin, *How the Idea of Religious Toleration Came to the West* (Princeton, NJ: Princeton University Press, 2003), p. 1.

[8] John Stuart Mill, *Auguste Comte and Positivism* (Ann Arbor: University of Michigan Press, 1961), p. 73.

[9] George H. Smith, *The System of Liberty: Themes in the History of Classical Liberalism* (New York: Cambridge/Cato Institute, 2013), p. 78.

[10] Lawrence Goldstone and Nancy Goldstone, *Out of the Flames: The Remarkable Story of a Fearless Scholar, a Fatal Heresy, and One of the Rarest Books in the World* (New York: Broadway, 2003), Kindle edition.

[11] Ibid., location 2620.

[12] Ibid., location 2277.

[13] Ibid.

[14] Ibid., location 2302.

[15] Ibid., location 2591.

[16] Bart D. Ehrman, *Lost Christianities: The Battles for Scripture and the Faiths We Never Knew* (New York: Oxford University Press, 2003), pp. 2–5.

[17] Zagorin, *Religious Toleration*, p. 22.

[18] Ibid., p. 25.

[19] Fourth Lateran Council: Canon 3 "On Heresy" (1215).

[20] Thomas Aquinas, *Summa Theologica*, II-II, Question 11, Article 3, Objection 3.

[21] Actually, Luther never said those words. He told the Holy Roman Emperor Charles V, "Unless I am convinced by the testimony of the Scriptures or by clear reason (for I do not trust either in the pope or in councils alone, since it is well known that they have often erred and contradicted themselves), I am bound by the Scriptures I have quoted and my conscience is captive to the Word of God. I cannot and will not recant anything, since it is neither safe nor right to go against conscience." After Luther's death, Georg Rörer, the first editor of his collected works, added the famous couplet—another in the long list of "famous quotes that were never said." Diarmaid MacCulloch, *Christianity: The First Three Thousand Years* (New York: Penguin, 2009), p. 611.

[22]Stefan Zweig, *The Right to Heresy: Castellio against Calvin* (Plunkett Lake Press; New York: Viking, 1936), Kindle edition.

[23]Ibid.

[24]Ibid., location 2659.

[25]Quoted in William Hamilton Drummond, *The Life of Michael Servetus* (London: John Chapman, 1848), p. 191.

[26]Zweig, *The Right to Heresy*, p. 1496.

[27]Ibid., p. 1650.

[28]Ibid., p. 1715.

[29]Quoted in Bruce Gordon, "To Kill a Heretic: Sebastian Castellio against John Calvin," in *Censorship Moments: Reading Texts in the History of Censorship and Freedom of Expression*, ed. Geoff Kemp (London: Bloomsbury Academic, 2014), p. 55.

[30]Sebastian Castellio, *Concerning heretics: whether they are to be persecuted and how they are to be treated; a collection of the opinions of learned men, both ancient and modern; an anonymous work*, trans. Roland Bainton (New York: Columbia University Press, 1935).

[31]Ibid.

[32]Ibid.

[33]Ibid.

[34]Ibid.

[35]Ibid.

[36]Ibid.

[37]Ibid.

[38]Ibid.

[39]Ibid.

[40]George H. Smith, "Religious Toleration versus Religious Freedom," Libertarianism.org, November 3, 2011, https://www.libertarianism.org/publications /essays/excursions/religious-toleration-versus-religious-freedom.

[41]John Milton, "Of True Religion, Heresy, Schism, Toleration: And What Best Means May Be Used against the Growth of Popery," *The Prose Works of John Milton*, vol. 2 (Philadelphia, PA: John W. Moore, 1847), http://oll.libertyfund.org /titles/milton-the-prose-works-of-john-milton-vol-2.

[42]John Locke, "Essay on Toleration," in *A Letter Concerning Toleration and Other Writings*, ed. Mark Goldie (Indianapolis, IN: Liberty Fund, 2010), p. 117.

[43]Ibid., p. 118.

[44]William Walwyn, "The Compassionate Samaritane," in *The Writings of William Walwyn*, ed. Jack R. McMichael and Barbara Taft (Athens: University of Georgia Press, 1989), p. 103.

[45]William Walwyn, "A New Petition of the Papists," in *Tracts on Liberty by the Levellers and their Critics*, vol. 1 (1638–1643), eds. David M. Hart and Ross Kenyon (Indianapolis, IN: Liberty Fund, 2015), http://oll.libertyfund.org /titles/2597#Leveller_1542-01-21May2015_389.

[46]Richard Price, *Observations on the Importance of the American Revolution, and the Means of Making It a Benefit to the World* (London: T. Cadell, 1785), pp. 34–35, http:// oll.libertyfund.org/titles/1788#Price_0894_42 (emphasis in original).

[47]Guido de Ruggiero, *The History of European Liberalism*, trans. R. G. Collingwood (Boston, MA: Beacon Press, 1959), p. 26.

[48]Walwyn, "A New Petition of the Papists."

Chapter 2

[1]See Douglas Laycock, "Religious Liberty and the Culture Wars," *University of Illinois Law Review* 2014, no. 3 (2014): 839; Douglas Laycock, "Sex, Atheism, and the Free Exercise of Religion," *University of Detroit Mercy Law Review* 88 (2011): 407.

[2]See, for example, Douglas Laycock, "Religious Liberty as Liberty," *Journal of Contemporary Legal Issues* 7, no. 2 (1996): 353.

[3]*Employment Division, Dep't of Human Resources of Or. v. Smith*, 494 U.S. 872 (1990).

[4]410 U.S. 113 (1973).

[5]See Douglas Laycock and Oliver S. Thomas, "Interpreting the Religious Freedom Restoration Act," *Texas Law Review* 73 (1994): 230–34, 236–38 (describing the pro-life opposition to RFRA); "What Hath Congress Wrought? An Interpretive Guide to the Religious Freedom Restoration Act," *Villanova Law Review* 39 (1994): 15–17 (same). These articles also review the law's enactment more generally.

[6]505 U.S. 83 (1992).

[7]See Douglas Laycock, "Religious Liberty for Politically Active Minority Groups: A Response to NeJaime and Siegel," *Yale Law Journal* 125 (2016): 375 (quoting this testimony).

[8]See Laycock and Thomas, "Interpreting the Religious Freedom Restoration Act," p. 210, n.9 (listing the organizations that were members of the Coalition for the Free Exercise of Religion).

[9]H.R. 4019 and S. 2148 in the 105th Congress, and H.R. 1691 and S. 2081 in the 106th Congress.

[10]See Laycock, "Sex, Atheism, and the Free Exercise of Religion," 412–13.

[11]See H. Rep. 106-219, pp. 34–37 (1999) (dissenting views).

[12]See Brief of Christian Legal Society et al., as Amici Curiae in Support of Hobby Lobby and Conestoga Wood 14–31, in *Burwell v. Hobby Lobby Stores, Inc.*, 134 S. Ct. 2751 (2014) (Nos. 13-354 and 13-356) (quoting Nadler Amendment in full and reviewing debate in detail).

[13]See Laycock, "Sex, Atheism, and the Free Exercise of Religion," 413n38 (collecting and categorizing the votes).

[14]See *Church of the Lukumi Babalu Aye, Inc. v. City of Hialeah*, 508 U.S. 520 (1993); *Employment Div. v. Smith*, 494 U.S. 872 (1990).

[15]See Douglas Laycock, "The Campaign against Religious Liberty," in *The Rise of Corporate Religious Liberty*, eds. Micah Schwartzman, Chad Flanders, and Zoe Robinson (New York: Oxford University Press, 2016), p. 248 (collecting these claims with citations).

[16]Ibid., pp. 253–54.

[17]*Burwell v. Hobby Lobby Stores, Inc.*, 134 S. Ct. 2751 (2014).

[18]*Zubik v. Burwell*, 136 S. Ct. 1557 (2016).

[19]See Brief of Baptist Joint Committee for Religious Liberty as Amicus Curiae in Support of Respondents, in *Zubik v. Burwell*, 136 S. Ct. 1557 2016 (No. 14-1418 et al.)

[20]The text of the Russell Amendment is available at http://docs.house.gov /meetings/AS/AS00/20160427/104832/BILLS-114-HR4909-R000604-Amdt-232r2 .pdf. The amendment works by reference to two existing statutory provisions that exempt only a "religious corporation, association, educational institution, or society." See 42 U.S.C. §2000e-1(a) (2012) and 42 U.S.C. 12113(d) (2012). They do not apply to "any person," the term that was held in *Hobby Lobby* to include for-profit corporations.

[21]The text of the Maloney Amendment is available at *Congressional Record* 162, no. 80 (May 19, 2016): H 2857.

[22]"Maloney Wants NDAA Veto If LGBT Amendment Included," *CQ News*, September 29, 2016.

[23]See, for example, Charles M. Blow, "Republican Self-Destruction," *New York Times*, March 28, 2016 ("so-called Religious Liberty Bill"); Erik Eckholm, "Next Fight for Gay Rights: Bias in Jobs and Housing," *New York Times*, June 27, 2015 ("'religious liberty' bills"); Jesse Wegman, "Religious Freedom and Political Lies in Indiana," *New York Times*, March 31, 2015 ("so-called 'religious freedom' laws"); Richard Fausset, "Religious Bias Issues Debated after Atlanta Mayor's Dismissal of Fire Chief," *New York Times*, January 11, 2015 ("so-called religious freedom law").

[24]The ACLU filed briefs in opposition to the religious liberty claims in *Zubik v. Burwell*, 136 S. Ct. 1557 (2016); *Burwell v. Hobby Lobby Stores, Inc.*, 134 S. Ct. 2751 (2014); and *Hosanna-Tabor Evangelical Lutheran Church & Sch. v. EEOC*, 132 S. Ct. 694 (2012). The religious liberty page of the ACLU's website is mostly devoted to explaining why religious liberty does not create exemptions with respect to health care, sexual orientation, or gender identity. See American Civil Liberties Union, "Religious Liberty," https://www.aclu.org/issues /religious-liberty.

[25]For development of the ideas in this paragraph, see Thomas C. Berg, "What Same-Sex Marriage and Religious-Liberty Claims Have in Common," *Northwestern Journal of Law and Social Policy* 5, no. 2 (2010): 212–27; see also William N. Eskridge, Jr., "A Jurisprudence of 'Coming Out': Religion, Homosexuality, and Collisions of Liberty and Equality in American Public Law," *Yale Law Journal* 106 (1997): 2416–30.

[26]On the deep mutual hostility of the two sides, see Laycock, "Religious Liberty and the Culture Wars," 869–71.

[27]Ibid., p. 877.

[28]See Laycock, "Religious Liberty for Politically Active Minority Groups," 378.

[29]403 U.S. 15 (1971).

[30]515 U.S. 557 (1995); see Laycock, "Religious Liberty for Politically Active Minority Groups," 376–78 (elaborating the point and collecting additional cases).

[31]Laycock, "Religious Liberty for Politically Active Minority Groups," 373n27 (collecting citations).

[32]See *Hively v. Ivy Tech Cmty. College*, 830 F.3d 698 (7th Cir. 2016) (reviewing this debate and the conflicting cases); *G.G. by Grimm v. Gloucester Cnty. Sch. Bd.*, 822 F.3d 709 (4th Cir.) (deferring to agency interpretation that the ban on sex discrimination prohibits discrimination based on claimant's preferred gender, without regard to biological sex), vacated; *Gloucester Cnty. Sch. Bd. v. G.G.*, No. 16-273, 2017 U.S. LEXIS 1626 (Mar. 6, 2017) (vacating the judgment and remanding for further consideration in light of new guidance document issued by the departments of Justice and Energy).

[33]2015 Utah L. ch. 13, codified in various sections of the Utah Antidiscrimination Act (Utah Code, Title 34A, ch. 5) and the Utah Fair Housing Act (Utah Code, Title 57, ch. 21).

[34]See, for example, Nelson Tebbe, Richard Schragger, and Micah Schwartzman, "Utah 'Compromise' to Protect LGBT Citizens from Discrimination Is No Model

for the Nation," *Outward* (blog), *Slate*, March 18, 2015, http://www.slate.com/blogs/outward/2015/03/18/gay_rights_the_utah_compromise_is_no_model_for_the_nation.html; Zack Ford, "Utah Bill Would Ban LGBT Discrimination, with Some Big Exceptions," *Think Progress*, March 6, 2015, http://thinkprogress.org/lgbt/2015/03/06/3630229/utah-lgbt-nondiscrimination-bill/.

[35]546 U.S. 418 (2006).

[36]132 S. Ct. 694 (2012).

[37]135 S. Ct. 853 (2015).

[38]See *Hosanna-Tabor*, 132 S. Ct. at 710.

[39]See, for example, *Holt v. Hobbs*, 135 S. Ct. 853 (2015) (amicus brief and oral argument in support of prisoner RLUIPA claim); *United States v. Secretary, Fla. Dep't of Corrections*, 828 F.3d 1341 (11th Cir. 2016) (government litigated claim to kosher meals in Florida prisons); *Ali v. Stephens*, 822 F.3d 776 (5th Cir. 2016) (amicus brief and oral argument in support of prisoner RLUIPA claim); *Chabad Lubavitch, Inc. v. Litchfield Historic Dist. Comm'n*, 768 F.3d 183 (2d Cir. 2014) (amicus brief in support of RLUIPA land use claim); *Bethel World Outreach Ministries v. Montgomery Cnty. Council*, 706 F.3d 548 (4th Cir. 2013) (amicus brief in support of RLUIPA land use claim); *Centro Familiar Cristiano Buenas Nuevas*, 651 F.3d 1163 (9th Cir. 2011) (amicus brief in support of RLUIPA land-use claim); U.S. Department of Justice, "Religious Land Use and Institutionalized Persons Act," https://www.justice.gov/crt/religious-land-use-and-institutionalized-persons-act (collecting department's statements and reports on RLUIPA's land-use provisions); U.S. Department of Justice, "Religious Land Use and Institutionalized Persons Act," https://www.justice.gov/crt/religious-land-use-and-institutionalized-persons-act-0 (collecting department's statements, reports, and briefs on RLUIPA's institutionalized-persons provisions).

[40]Executive Order 13279, *Federal Register* 67 (December 12, 2002): 77141.

[41]"Application of the Religious Freedom Restoration Act to the Award of a Grant Pursuant to the Juvenile Justice and Delinquency Prevention Act," *Opinions of the Office of Legal Counsel* 31 (June 29, 2007): 162, https://www.justice.gov/olc/opinions-main.

[42]There were repeated letters to the Attorney General from interest groups and legislators; I believe that those remain unpublished. For published demands for withdrawal, see Columbia Law School Public Rights/Private Conscience Project, *Law Professors' Analysis of a Need for Legal Guidance and Policy-Making on Religious Exemptions Raised by Federal Contractors*, May 10, 2016, http://web.law.columbia.edu/gender-sexuality/public-rights-private-conscience-project/policy. See also Melissa Rogers, Chair, President's Advisory Council on Faith-Based and Neighborhood Partnerships, Testimony on Faith-Based Initiatives: Recommendations of the President's Advisory Council on Faith-Based and Community Partnerships and Other Current Issues, before the Subcommittee on the Constitution, Civil Rights, and Civil Liberties of the House Committee on the Judiciary, 111th Cong., 2nd sess., November 18, 2010, pp. 24–33, https://www.gpo.gov/fdsys/pkg/CHRG-111hhrg62343/pdf/CHRG-111hhrg62343.pdf. In the same hearing, see the testimony of Barry W. Lynn, Executive Director, Americans United for Separation of Church and State, pp. 56–59, 64–68; and see also the very hostile questioning on the employment issue by Democratic legislators, pp. 145–62.

[43]134 S. Ct. 1811 (2014).

Chapter 3

[1]Peter J. Gomes, "Best Sermon; A Pilgrim's Progress," *New York Times Magazine*, April 18, 1999, http://www.nytimes.com/1999/04/18/magazine/best-sermon-a -pilgrim-s-progress.html.

[2]Quoted in Baptist Wriothesley Noel, *Essay on the Union of Church and State* (London: James Nisbet and Co., 1848), p. 56.

[3]John M. Barry, "God, Government and Roger Williams' Big Idea," *Smithsonian Magazine*, January 2012, http://www.smithsonianmag.com/history /god-government-and-roger-williams-big-idea-6291280/.

[4]Roger Williams to Anne Sadleir, April 1652, in *The Correspondence of Roger Williams*, vol. 2, ed. Glenn W. LaFantasie (Providence, RI: Brown University Press/ University Press of New England, Hanover and London, 1988).

[5]Gordon J. Schochet, ed., *Religion, Resistance, and Civil War* (Washington: Folger Institute, 1990), p. 131.

[6]Wallace Notestein and Frances Helen Relf, eds., *Commons Debates for 1629*, vol. 10–11 (Minneapolis: University of Minnesota, 1921), pp. 18–19.

[7]James E. Ernst, *Roger Williams: New England Firebrand* (London: McMillan Company, 1932), p. 90.

[8]Matt. 13:24–30.

[9]William G. McLoughlin, *New England Dissent, 1630–1833: The Baptists and the Separation of Church and State*, vol. 1 (Cambridge, MA: Harvard University Press, 1971), p. 7.

[10]Roger Williams, *The Complete Writings of Roger Williams, Vol. 3: Bloudy Tenent of Persecution* (Eugene, OR: Wipf and Stock Publishers, 2007).

[11]James Kendall Hosmer, ed., *Winthrop's Journal: History of New England*, vol. 2 (New York: Charles Scribner's Sons, 1908), pp. 237–39.

[12]Williams, *Bloudy Tenent of Persecution*, p. 398.

[13]Robert Baillie, "Anabaptism: The Fountain of Independency," in James Ernst, *Roger Williams and the English Revolution*, vol. 1 (Providence: Rhode Island Historical Society Collections, 1931).

[14]David Little, "Conscience, Theology and the First Amendment," *Soundings* 72, no. 2/3 (Summer/Fall 1989): 357–78.

[15]Winthrop Hudson, "John Locke: Heir of Puritan Political Theorists," in *Calvinism and the Political Order*, ed. George Hunt (London: The Westminster Press, 1965), pp. 117–18.

[16]W. K. Jordan, *The Development of Religious Toleration in England*, vol. 3 (Cambridge, MA: Harvard University Press, 1965), p. 475.

Chapter 4

[1]Martin Luther King, Jr., to Fellow Clergymen, "Letter from a Birmingham Jail," April 16, 1963.

Chapter 7

[1]Charles L. Glenn, *Educational Freedom in Eastern Europe* (Washington: Cato Institute, 1995).

[2]Jacques Maritain, *The Person and the Common Good*, trans. John J. Fitzgerald (Notre Dame, IN: University of Notre Dame Press, 1996), p. 3.

[3]Steven V. Monsma, *Pluralism and Freedom: Faith-Based Organizations in a Democratic Society* (Lanham, MD: Rowman and Littlefield, 2012), p. 123.

[4]John E. Coons, "Intellectual Liberty and the Schools," *Notre Dame Journal of Law, Ethics, & Public Policy* 1, no. 4 (1985): 511.

[5]Peter L. Berger, "The Serendipity of Liberties," in *The Structure of Freedom: Correlations, Causes, and Causation*, ed. John Neuhaus (Grand Rapids, MI: Eerdmans, 1991), p. 15.

[6]Ibid.

[7]James Madison, *Memorial and Remonstrance against Religious Assessment*, ed. Jack Rakove (New York: Library of America, 1999), p. 30.

[8]Jonathan Zimmerman, *Whose America? Culture Wars in the Public School* (Cambridge, MA: Harvard University Press, 2002), p. 189.

[9]Charles L. Glenn, *The Myth of the Common School* (Amherst: University of Massachusetts Press, 1988).

[10]Charles L. Glenn, *The American Model of State and School* (London: Bloomsbury Academic, 2012).

[11]Mark Holmes, "Education and Citizenship in an Age of Pluralism," in *Making Good Citizens: Education and Civil Society*, ed. Diane Ravitch and Joseph P. Viteritti (New Haven, CT: Yale University Press, 2001), p. 205.

[12]Alan Peshkin, *God's Choice: The Total World of a Fundamentalist Christian School* (Chicago: University of Chicago Press, 1986).

Chapter 9

[1]Portions of this chapter are drawn from Charles C. Haynes, "Religious Liberty in the Public Schools: Toward a Common Vision for the Common Good," in *Religious Freedom in America: Constitutional Roots and Contemporary Challenges*, ed. Allen D. Hertzke (Norman: University of Oklahoma Press, 2015).

[2]For the text of the consensus guidelines discussed in this chapter, see Charles C. Haynes and Oliver Thomas, *Finding Common Ground: A First Amendment Guide to Religion and Public Schools* (Nashville, TN: First Amendment Center, 2011), http://www.religiousfreedomcenter.org/wp-content/uploads/2014/08/rfc_publications_findingcommonground.pdf.

Chapter 11

[1]Steven K. Green, *The Second Disestablishment: Church and State in Nineteenth-Century America* (New York: Oxford University Press, 2010).

[2]See http://tonyblairfaithfoundation.org/sites/default/files/Essentials%20of%20Dialogue%20For%20Distribution.pdf.

Chapter 12

[1]See John M. Barry, "The Opening Argument: Church, State, and the Birth of Liberty," in this volume.

[2]Brief for Cato Institute as Amicus Curiae at 34, *Obergefell v. Hodges*, 135 S. Ct. 2584 (2015) (14-556). Twelve years earlier, the Supreme Court cited Cato's brief twice in its opinion in *Lawrence v. Texas*, which overturned a Texas statute that criminalized same-sex sodomy: Brief for the Cato Institute as Amicus Curiae, *Lawrence v. Texas*, 539 U.S. 558 (2003) (02-102), https://www.cato.org/publications

/legal-briefs/lawrence-v-texas. I discussed the *Obergefell* ruling in some detail in Roger Pilon, "Foreword," *2014–2015 Cato Supreme Court Review* vii (2015): xiii–xxi.

[3]Not only is the couple's religious liberty at issue in this still-ongoing litigation, but the court has imposed a gag order on the couple, thus implicating their speech rights as well. "Christian Bakers Who Refused to Serve Lesbians Appeal Fine," FoxNews.com, March 2, 2017, http://video.foxnews.com /v/5346020550001/?#sp=show-clips.

[4]This case has now been decided, but the opinion has yet to be officially published. *State v. Arlene's Flowers, Inc.*, No. 91615-2, 2017 Wash. LEXIS 216 (February 16, 2017).

[5]Roger Pilon, "Whatever Happened to Religious Freedom?" *Wall Street Journal*, July 13, 2015, https://www.wsj.com/articles/whatever-happened-to-religious -freedom-1436827114.

[6]Jonathan Scruggs, "Attorney Explains Why Phoenix Artists Are Suing Rather Than Create Art for Same-Sex Weddings," *AZ Central*, June 3, 2016, http:// www.azcentral.com/story/opinion/op-ed/2016/06/03/same-sex-marriage -lawsuit/85211088/.

[7]Kenneth C. Davis, "America's True History of Religious Tolerance," *Smithsonian Magazine*, October 2010, http://www.smithsonianmag.com/history/americas -true-history-of-religious-tolerance-61312684/; Chris Beneke and Christopher S. Grenda, ed., *The First Prejudice: Religious Tolerance and Intolerance in Early America* (Philadelphia: University of Pennsylvania Press, 2011), pp. 3–4.

[8]Maria Mayo, "Religion in America on July 4, 1776," *The Huffington Post*, July 4, 2014, http://www.huffingtonpost.com/maria-mayo/religion-in-america-on-july -4-1776_b_3542203.html.

[9]U.S. Constitution, art. 6, cl. 3.

[10]U.S. Constitution, amend. 1.

[11]*Everson v. Board of Education*, 330 U.S. 1, 14–16 (1947) (applying the Establishment Clause to the states); *Cantwell v. State of Connecticut*, 310 U.S. 296, 303 (1940) (applying the Free Exercise Clause). The Bill of Rights applied originally only against the federal government (*Barron v. Baltimore*, 32 U.S. [7 Pet.] 243 [1833]); but with the ratification of the Fourteenth Amendment in 1868, most of those rights became good against the states as well, although they would be "incorporated" against the states only on a case-by-cases basis over time.

[12]See Edward S. Corwin, *The "Higher Law" Background of American Constitutional Law* (Indianapolis, IN: Liberty Fund, 2003).

[13]*Robert v. U.S. Jaycees*, 468 U.S. 609, 623 (stating "freedom of association therefore plainly presupposes a freedom not to associate").

[14]Roger Pilon, "Has Freedom of Association Become a Crime?" *The National Interest*, April 4, 2015, http://nationalinterest.org/feature/when-did-freedom -association-become-crime-12547.

[15]Joseph William Singer, "No Right to Exclude: Public Accommodations and Private Property," *Northwestern University Law Review* 90 (Summer 1996): 1304–11.

[16]Charles W. Baird, "On Freedom of Association," *FEE*, July, 1, 2002, https://fee .org/articles/on-freedom-of-association/.

[17]Richard Epstein, "Freedom of Association and Antidiscrimination Law: An Imperfect Reconciliation," *Library of Law and Liberty*, January 2, 2016,

http://www.libertylawsite.org/liberty-forum/freedom-of-association-and
-antidiscrimination-law-an-imperfect-reconciliation/.

[18]Pilon, "Has Freedom of Association Become a Crime?"

[19]Roger Pilon, "Freedom of Association Takes Another Hit," *Cato at Liberty*, February 16, 2017, https://www.cato.org/blog/freedom-association-takes-another-hit.

[20]*Employment Div., Dept. of Human Resources of Oregon v. Smith*, 494 U.S. 872, 879 (1990).

[21]*Burwell v. Hobby Lobby Stores, Inc.*, 134 S. Ct. 2751, 2761 (2014).

[22]Howard M. Friedman, "10 Things You Need to Know to Really Understand RFRA in Indiana and Arkansas," *Washington Post*, April 1, 2015, https://www.washingtonpost.com/news/acts-of-faith/wp/2015/04/01/10-things-you-need-to-know-to-really-understand-rfra-in-indiana-and-arkansas/?utm_term=.d6f5a6896704.

[23]Emma Green, "Can States Protect LGBT Rights without Compromising Religious Freedom?" *The Atlantic*, January 6, 2016, https://www.theatlantic.com/politics/archive/2016/01/lgbt-discrimination-protection-states-religion/422730/.

[24]Religious Freedom Restoration Act: Congressional Finding and Declaration of Finding, 42 U.S.C. § 2000bb (1993).

[25]Roger Pilon, "We're Not 'All in This Together' Mr. Obama, and We Don't Want Obamacare," *Forbes*, October 17, 2013, https://www.cato.org/publications/commentary/were-not-all-together-mr-obama-we-dont-want-obamacare.

[26]Roger Pilon, "How the Bishops Undermined Individual Responsibility," *Daily Caller*, February 15, 2012, https://www.cato.org/publications/commentary/how-bishops-undermined-individual-responsibility.

[27]Neal McCluskey, "Should the Feds Decide the Transgender Bathroom Issue?" *Daily Caller*, May 17, 2016, http://dailycaller.com/2016/05/17/should-the-feds-decide-the-transgender-bathroom-issue/.

[28]Fewer than 1 percent of students identify with a gender different than their biological and genetic gender. Jan Hoffman, "As Attention Grows, Transgender Children's Numbers Are Elusive," *New York Times*, May 17, 2016, https://www.nytimes.com/2016/07/01/health/transgender-population.html.

[29]Jason Bedrick, "On Religious Liberty, the Bathroom Wars, and Educational Choice," *Ricochet*, May 16, 2016, https://ricochet.com/archives/religious-liberty-bathroom-wars-educational-choice/.

[30]James Esseks, "Talking Points on Ed/DOJ Guidance on Title IX," ACLU, June 2016, http://www.aclu-il.org/wp-content/uploads/2016/06/Esseks-Talking-points-on-ED-DOJ-Guidance-on-Title-IX.pdf.

Chapter 13

[1]515 U.S. 557 (1995).
[2]562 U.S. 443 (2011).
[3]135 S. Ct. 2584 (2015).

Chapter 14

[1]The harms may have added dimensions in other contexts, such as when hospitals and other health care institutions seek exemptions that would result in people being denied critical health care.

[2]511 U.S. 127, 142 (1994).

[3]*Obergefell v. Hodges*, 135 S. Ct. 2584, 2602 (2015).

[4]*Heart of Atlanta Motel, Inc. v. United States*, 379 U.S. 241, 291–92 (1964) (Goldberg, J., concurring) (quoting S. Rep. No. 88-872, at 16 (1964)).

[5]*Newman v. Piggie Park Enter., Inc.*, 256 F. Supp. 941, 945 (D.S.C. 1966).

[6]*Bob Jones Univ. v. United States*, 461 U.S. 574, 604 (1983).

Chapter 15

[1]Randy E. Barnett, *Our Republican Constitution: Securing the Liberty and Sovereignty of We the People* (New York: Broadside Books, 2016).

[2]Sherif Girgis, Ryan T. Anderson, and Robert P. George, *What Is Marriage?: Man and Woman: A Defense* (New York: Encounter Books, 2012).

[3]Nebraska lifted the ban in 2017. See, "Nebraska Ends Ban on Religious Garb in Public Schools," *Chicago Tribune*, March 27, 2017, http://www.chicagotribune .com/news/nationworld/ct-nebraska-ban-religious-garb-20170327-story .html.

Chapter 16

[1]Alexis de Tocqueville, *Democracy in America: Historical-Critical Edition of De la démocratie en Amérique*, ed. Eduardo Nolla, trans. from the French by James T. Schleifer. A Bilingual French-English edition (Indianapolis: Liberty Fund, 2010). vol. 2., p. 479.

[2]Ibid.

[3]Ibid., p. 480.

[4]See U.S. Constitution, art. 6, cl. 3.

[5]See U.S. Constitution, amend. 1.

[6]*Everson v. Bd. of Educ. of Ewing Twp.*, 330 U.S. 1, 8 (1947); *Cantwell v. Connecticut*, 310 U.S. 296, 303 (1940).

[7]*Employment Division v. Smith*, 494 U.S. 872 (1990).

[8]Ibid., pp. 874, 890.

[9]Ibid., p. 879.

[10]Ibid., p. 894 (O'Connor, J., concurring).

[11]See Religious Freedom Restoration Act, 42 U.S.C. § 2000bb–1 (2012).

[12]"H.R.1308–Religious Freedom Restoration Act of 1993," Congress.gov, https:// www.congress.gov/bill/103rd-congress/house-bill/1308/actions.

[13]Peter Steinfels, "Clinton Signs Law Protecting Religious Practices," *New York Times*, November 17, 1993, http://www.nytimes.com/1993/11/17/us/clinton -signs-law-protecting-religious-practices.html.

[14]Ibid.

[15]*Congressional Record* 139 (May 11, 1993): H 2363 (statement of Rep. Pelosi).

[16]Ibid.

[17]Ibid., H 2359 (statement of Rep. Nadler).

[18]President William Clinton, "Remarks on Signing the Religious Freedom Restoration Act of 1993" (Speech, Washington, November 16, 1993).

[19]*City of Boerne v. Flores*, 521 U.S. 507 (1997).

[20]Ibid., pp. 511, 544.

[21]See Alabama Constitution, amend. 622.

[22]Protection of Land Use as Religious Exercise, 42 U.S.C. §§ 2000cc. (2012).

[23]Louise Melling, "ACLU: Why We Can No Longer Support the Federal 'Religious Freedom' Law," *Washington Post*, June 25, 2015, https://www.washingtonpost.com/opinions/congress-should-amend-the-abused-religious-freedom-restoration-act/2015/06/25/ee6aaa46-19d8-11e5-ab92-c75ae6ab94b5_story.html?postshare=6371435345896586.

[24]Barry W. Lynn, "First, Do No Harm: How to Restore a Federal Religious Freedom Act," *Wall of Separation* (blog), May 18, 2016, https://www.au.org/blogs/wall-of-separation/first-do-no-harm-how-to-restore-a-federal-religious-freedom-law.

[25]Martin S. Lederman, "Reconstructing RFRA: The Contested Legacy of Religious Freedom Restoration," *Yale Law Journal Forum* 125 (March 2016): 418.

[26]Michael W. McConnell, "The Origins and Historical Understanding of Free Exercise of Religion," *Harvard Law Review* 103, no. 7 (May 1990): 1420.

[27]Gerard V. Bradley, "Beguiled: Free Exercise Exemptions and the Siren Song of Liberalism," *Hofstra Law Review* 20, no. 2 (Winter 1991): 248.

[28]Philip A. Hamburger, "A Constitutional Right of Religious Exemption: An Historical Perspective," *George Washington Law Review* 60, no. 4 (April 1992): 917.

[29]Eugene Volokh, "Why I Agree Both with *Smith* and with RFRA," *The Volokh Conspiracy*, October 31, 2005, http://volokh.com/2005/10/31/why-i-agree-both-with-smith-and-with-rfra/.

[30]*Smith*, 494 U.S. at 890.

[31]Samuel Warren and Louis Brandeis, "The Right to Privacy," *Harvard Law Review* 4, no. 5 (December 1890): 193.

[32]*Olmstead v. United States*, 277 U.S. 438 (1928).

[33]Ibid., p. 478 (Brandeis, J., dissenting).

[34]James Madison to the Honorable the General Assembly of the Commonwealth of Virginia, "Memorial and Remonstrance against Religious Assessments," June 20, 1785, http://press-pubs.uchicago.edu/founders/documents/amendI_religions43.html.

[35]James Madison, "Property," *National Gazette*, March 29, 1792.

[36]Thomas Jefferson, "A Bill for Establishing Religious Freedom," June 18, 1779, https://founders.archives.gov/documents/Jefferson/01-02-02-0132-0004-0082.

[37]Delaware Declaration of Rights § 2 (Del. 1776).

[38]Pennsylvania Constitution of 1776, part 1, art. 2 (superseded 1790).

[39]Massachusetts Constitution, part 1, art. 2.

[40]An Act for Establishing Religious Freedom, Virginia General Assembly (passed January 16, 1786).

[41]*Church of the Lukumi Babalu Aye v. City of Hialeah*, 508 U.S. 520 (1993).

[42]Ibid., pp. 542, 546.

[43]Ibid., p. 547.

[44]*Smith*, 494 U.S. at 890.

[45]*Gonzales v. O Centro Espirita Beneficente Uniao Do Vegetal*, 546 U.S. 418 (2006).

[46]Gaillard Hunt, ed., *Journals of the Continental Congress 1774–1789*, vol. 25 (Washington: Government Printing Office, 1992), pp. 819, 825–26.

[47]Secretary of State James Madison to Bishop John Carroll, November 20, 1806 (on file with the National Archives).

[48]Memorandum from President James Madison to the House of Representatives, February 21, 1811 (on file with the University of Virginia Miller Center).

[49]*Watson v. Jones*, 80 U.S. 679 (1872).

[50]Ibid., pp. 717, 735.

[51]Ibid., p. 727.

[52]*Kedroff v. Saint Nicholas Cathedral of the Russian Orthodox Church in North America*, 344 U.S. 94 (1952).

[53]Ibid., p. 115.

[54]*Serbian Eastern Orthodox Diocese for United States and Canada v. Milivojevich*, 426 U.S. 696 (1976).

[55]Ibid., p. 698.

[56]Ibid., p. 724.

[57]*Hosanna-Tabor Evangelical Lutheran Church & School v. EEOC*, 132 S. Ct. 694 (2012).

[58]Ibid., pp. 702, 710.

[59]Ibid., pp. 706, 709.

[60]Ibid., p. 707.

[61]U.S. Constitution, art. 6, cl. 3.

[62]U.S. Constitution, art. 2, § 1, cl. 8.

[63]McConnell, "Origins and Historical Understanding of Free Exercise of Religion."

[64]Resolution of July 18, 1775, reprinted in Worthington Chauncey Ford, ed., *Journals of the Continental Congress 1774–1789*, vol. 2 (Washington: Government Printing Office, 1905), pp. 187, 189.

[65]McConnell, "Origins and Historical Understanding of Free Exercise of Religion," p. 1469.

[66]N.Y. Ct. Gen. Sess. (unpublished 1813), reprinted in T. Walker, ed., "The People v. Daniel Philips and Wife," *Western Law Journal* 1, no. 3 (December 1843): 109.

[67]N.Y. Rev. Stat., pt. III, ch. VII, tit. 3, art. 8, § 72 (1828).

[68]*Pierce v. Society of the Sisters of the Holy Names of Jesus and Mary*, 268 U.S. 510 (1925).

[69]Ibid., p. 535.

[70]Ibid., pp. 530–33.

[71]Ibid., pp. 534–35.

[72]Ibid., p. 534.

[73]Ibid.

[74]Ibid., p. 535.

[75]*West Virginia State Board of Education v. Barnette*, 319 U.S. 624 (1943).

[76]Ibid., pp. 628–29, 642.

[77]Ibid., p. 628.

[78]Ibid., pp. 625, 642.

[79]Ibid., p. 642.

[80]Ibid., p. 630.

[81]Ibid., p. 631.

[82]Ibid., p. 644 (Black, J., concurring).

[83]Ibid.

[84]Ibid., p. 651 (Frankfurter, J., dissenting).

[85]Ibid., p. 656 (Frankfurter, J., dissenting) (citing *Pierce*, 268 U.S. 510).

[86]Ibid., pp. 646–47 (Frankfurter, J., dissenting).

[87]See, generally, William H. Pryor Jr., "The Religious Faith and Judicial Duty of an American Catholic Judge," *Yale Law and Policy Review* 24, no. 2 (Spring 2006): 347.

[88]James L. Buckley, "The Catholic Public Servant," *First Things*, February 1992, https://www.firstthings.com/article/1992/02/002-the-catholic-public-servant.

[89]*Catechism of the Catholic Church*, 2nd ed. (Washington: United States Conference of Catholic Bishops, 2000), ¶ 1749. (Emphasis added.)

[90]Germain Grisez, *The Way of the Lord Jesus: Difficult Moral Questions,* vol. 3 (San Jose, CA: Franciscan Press, 1997), pp. 871–97.

[91]*Catechism of the Catholic Church,* ¶ 1750.

[92]Ibid., ¶ 1755. (Emphasis in the original.)

[93]Ibid., ¶ 1753.

[94]Grisez, *The Way of the Lord Jesus,* p. 873.

[95]Ibid.

[96]Ibid.

[97]Ibid., pp. 876–89.

[98]*Catechism of the Catholic Church,* ¶ 2284.

[99]Ibid., ¶ 2287.

[100]Ibid., ¶ 2286.

[101]Ibid., ¶ 2285.

[102]John H. Garvey and Amy V. Coney, "Catholic Judges in Capital Cases," *Marquette Law Review* 81, no. 2 (Winter 1998): 328; see also Stephen F. Smith, "Cultural Change and 'Catholic Lawyers,'" *Ave Maria Law Review* 1 (2003): 44.

[103]Justice Antonin Scalia, "Saint Thomas Aquinas and Law," Remarks at the Dominican House of Studies 800th Jubilee of the Order of Preachers, Washington, January 7, 2016.

[104]Ilya Shapiro, "Hobby Lobby and the Future of Freedom," *National Affairs* 23 (Spring 2015): 134. (Emphasis in the original.)

[105]Ibid.

[106]Megan McArdle, "Who's the Real Hobby Lobby Bully?," *BloombergView,* July 7, 2014, https://www.bloomberg.com/view/articles/2014-07-07/who-s-the-real -hobby-lobby-bully.

[107]Madison, "Property."

[108]Jefferson, "Establishing Religious Freedom."

[109]*Olmstead,* 277 U.S. at 478 (Brandeis, J., dissenting).

Chapter 17

[1]*Burwell v. Hobby Lobby Stores, Inc.,* 134 S. Ct. 2751 (2014). *Zubik v. Burwell,* 136 S. Ct. 1557 (2016).

[2]McArdle, "Who's the Real Hobby Lobby Bully?"

[3]Ibid.

[4]*Burwell* 134 S. Ct. at 2805 (2014) (Ginsburg, J., dissenting).

Index

Note: Information in notes is indicated by n.

Contributors

Doug Bandow

Doug Bandow is a senior fellow at the Cato Institute, specializing in foreign policy and civil liberties. He worked as special assistant to President Ronald Reagan and editor of the political magazine *Inquiry*. He writes regularly for leading publications such as *Fortune* magazine, *National Interest*, the *Wall Street Journal*, and the *Washington Times*. Bandow speaks frequently at academic conferences, on college campuses, and to business groups. Bandow has been a regular commentator on ABC, CBS, NBC, CNN, Fox News, and MSNBC. He holds a JD from Stanford University.

John M. Barry

John M. Barry is a prizewinning *New York Times* bestselling author, whose newest book—*Roger Williams and the Creation of the American Soul: Church, State, and the Birth of Liberty*—focuses on the development of both the idea of the separation of church and state and the first expression of individualism in a modern sense. His articles have appeared in such scientific journals as *Nature* and *Journal of Infectious Disease*, as well as such lay publications as *Sports Illustrated*, *Politico*, the *New York Times*, the *Washington Post*, and others. He is a frequent guest on broadcast networks and appears on such shows as *Meet the Press*, *World News*, and *All Things Considered*. He has also served as a consultant for Sony Pictures and contributed to award-winning television documentaries.

Trevor Burrus

Trevor Burrus is a research fellow at the Cato Institute's Center for Constitutional Studies and managing editor of the *Cato Supreme*

Court Review. His research interests include constitutional law, civil and criminal law, legal and political philosophy, and legal history. His academic work has appeared in journals such as the *Harvard Journal of Law and Public Policy*, the *New York University Journal of Law and Liberty*, the *New York University Annual Survey of American Law*, the *Syracuse Law Review*, and many others. His popular writing has appeared in the *Washington Post*, the *New York Times*, *USA Today*, *Forbes*, the *Huffington Post*, the *New York Daily News*, and others.

Burrus lectures regularly on behalf of the Federalist Society, the Institute for Humane Studies, the Foundation for Economics Education, and other organizations; and he frequently appears on major media outlets. He is also the cohost of *Free Thoughts*, a weekly podcast that covers topics in libertarian theory, history, and philosophy.

He is the editor of *A Conspiracy against Obamacare* (Palgrave Macmillan, 2013), and he holds a BA in philosophy from the University of Colorado at Boulder and a JD from the University of Denver Sturm College of Law.

Robert P. George

Professor George holds Princeton's celebrated McCormick Chair in Jurisprudence and is the founding director of the James Madison Program in American Ideals and Institutions. He served as chairman of the United States Commission on International Religious Freedom; before that, he served on the President's Council on Bioethics and as a presidential appointee to the United States Commission on Civil Rights. He also served as the U.S. member of UNESCO's World Commission on the Ethics of Scientific Knowledge and Technology. He is a former judicial fellow at the Supreme Court of the United States, where he received the Justice Tom C. Clark Award.

He is the author of numerous books on law and religion, and his scholarly articles and reviews have appeared in such journals as the *Harvard Law Review,* the *Yale Law Journal,* the *Columbia Law Review,* the *American Journal of Jurisprudence,* and the *Review of Politics.*

Professor George is a recipient of many honors and awards, including the Presidential Citizens Medal, the Honorific Medal for the Defense of Human Rights of the Republic of Poland, the Canterbury Medal of the Becket Fund for Religious Liberty, the Sidney Hook Memorial Award of the National Association of Scholars, the Philip Merrill Award of the American Council of Trustees and Alumni, the Bradley Prize for Intellectual and Civic Achievement, and Princeton University's President's Award for Distinguished Teaching. He has given honorific lectures at Harvard, Yale, University of St. Andrews, and Cornell University. He is a member of the Council on Foreign Relations, and he holds honorary doctorates of law, ethics, science, letters, divinity, humanities, law and moral values, civil law, humane letters, and juridical science. A graduate of Swarthmore College, he holds JD and MTS degrees from Harvard University and the degree of DPhil from Oxford University. In November 2016, he received the degrees of BCL and DCL from Oxford.

Charles L. Glenn

Charles L. Glenn is professor emeritus of educational leadership at Boston University, teaching courses in education history and U.S. and comparative policy. From 1970 to 1991, he was director of urban education and equity efforts for the Massachusetts Department of Education, including administration of more than $200 million in state funds for magnet schools and desegregation, and initial responsibility for the nation's first state bilingual education mandate and the law forbidding race and sex discrimination in education. His research in Europe and North America focuses on urban schooling, parental choice, schooling of linguistic and racial minority pupils, religion and education, history and sociology of education, reconciling national standards with school autonomy and distinctiveness, school desegregation, and equity. He is vice president of an international organization promoting educational freedom and the right to education, and he serves on the Massachusetts Advisory Committee to the U.S. Commission on Civil Rights. He holds an AB and EdD from Harvard and a PhD from Boston University.

Charles C. Haynes

Charles C. Haynes is the vice president of the Newseum Institute and executive director of the Religious Freedom Center. He is a senior scholar at the First Amendment Center. He actively speaks and writes to promote religious freedom in America. In addition to his nationally run newspaper column *Inside the First Amendment*, he is the coauthor of six books, including *Religion in American Public Life: Living with Our Deepest Differences* (2001), *First Freedoms: A Documentary History of First Amendment Rights in America* (2006), and *Finding Common Ground: A First Amendment Guide to Religion and Public Schools* (2014). Haynes was given the Virginia First Freedom Award from the Council for America's First Freedom in 2008. He received his master's degree from Harvard Divinity School and his doctorate from Emory University.

Douglas Laycock

Douglas Laycock is perhaps the nation's leading authority on the law of religious liberty and also on the law of remedies. He has taught and written about these topics for four decades at the University of Chicago, the University of Texas, the University of Michigan, and now the University of Virginia.

Laycock has testified frequently before Congress and has argued many cases in the courts, including the U.S. Supreme Court. He is the author of the leading casebook *Modern American Remedies*, the award-winning monograph *The Death of the Irreparable Injury Rule*, and many articles in the leading law reviews. He coedited a collection of essays, *Same-Sex Marriage and Religious Liberty*.

His many writings on religious liberty are being published in a five-volume collection. *Religious Liberty, Volume One: Overviews and History* and *Volume Two: The Free Exercise Clause* have been published. *Volume Three: Religious Freedom Restoration Acts and Same-Sex Marriage Legislation, Volume Four: Federal Religious Liberty Legislation after RFRA*, and *Volume Five: The Free Speech and Establishment Clauses* are forthcoming.

Laycock is vice president of the American Law Institute and a fellow of the American Academy of Arts and Sciences. He earned his BA from Michigan State University and his JD from the University of Chicago Law School.

Neal McCluskey

Neal McCluskey is the director of Cato's Center for Educational Freedom. Before arriving at Cato, McCluskey served in the U.S. Army, taught high school English, and was a freelance reporter covering municipal government and education in suburban New Jersey.

More recently, he was a policy analyst at the Center for Education Reform. McCluskey is the author of the book *Feds in the Classroom: How Big Government Corrupts, Cripples, and Compromises American Education*, and his writings have appeared in such publications as the *Wall Street Journal*, the *Washington Post*, and *Forbes*. In addition to his written work, McCluskey has appeared on C-SPAN, CNN, Fox News, and numerous radio programs.

McCluskey holds an undergraduate degree from Georgetown University, where he double-majored in government and English; he has a master's degree in political science from Rutgers University and a PhD in public policy from George Mason University.

David McDonald

David McDonald is a legal associate in the Cato Institute's Center for Constitutional Studies. During law school, he interned for the New York State Supreme Court's Commercial Division and clerked for the Institute for Justice, a public interest law firm in Arlington, Virginia. McDonald holds a JD from Columbia Law School, where he served as an articles editor for the *Columbia Business Law Review*. He holds a BA in political science from the University of California, Los Angeles.

Louise Melling

Louise Melling is a deputy legal director of the American Civil Liberties Union (ACLU) and director of its Center for Liberty. The center encompasses the ACLU's work on reproductive freedom; women's rights; lesbian, gay, bisexual, and transgender rights; and freedom of religion and belief. Previously, Melling was director of the ACLU Reproductive Freedom Project, in which capacity she oversaw nationwide litigation, communications research, public education campaigns, and advocacy efforts in the state legislatures. Melling has appeared in federal and state courts around the country to challenge laws that restrict reproductive rights. She has appeared in many media outlets, including CNN, PBS News Hour, Frontline, the *New York Times*, the *Washington Post*, and *USA Today*. Melling holds a BA from Oberlin College and a JD from Yale Law School.

Roger Pilon

Roger Pilon is the founding director of Cato's Center for Constitutional Studies, which has become an important force in the national debate over constitutional interpretation and judicial philosophy. He is also the founding publisher of the *Cato Supreme Court Review* and the inaugural holder of Cato's B. Kenneth Simon Chair in Constitutional Studies.

Before joining Cato, Pilon held five senior posts in the Reagan administration, including positions at the Departments of State and Justice, and was a national fellow at Stanford's Hoover Institution. In 1989, the Bicentennial Commission presented him with its Benjamin Franklin Award for excellence in writing on the U.S. Constitution. In 2001, Columbia University's School of General Studies awarded him its Alumni Medal of Distinction. Pilon lectures and debates at universities and law schools across the country and testifies often before Congress.

His writing has appeared in the *Wall Street Journal*, the *Washington Post*, the *New York Times*, the *Los Angeles Times*, *Legal Times*, the *National Law Journal*, the *Harvard Journal of Law and Public Policy*, the *Stanford Law and Policy Review*, and elsewhere. He has appeared on ABC's *Nightline*, CBS's *60 Minutes II*, Fox News, NPR, CNN, MSNBC, CNBC, C-SPAN, and other media.

Pilon holds a BA from Columbia University, an MA and a PhD from the University of Chicago, and a JD from the George Washington University School of Law.

Hon. William H. Pryor Jr.

William H. Pryor Jr. is a judge on the U.S. Court of Appeals for the Eleventh Circuit. Initially appointed by President George W. Bush during a Senate recess in 2004, Judge Pryor's appointment was confirmed by the U.S. Senate in 2005.

Judge Pryor served as attorney general of Alabama from 1997 to 2004. When first appointed, he was the youngest attorney general in the nation. He was later elected and reelected to that office in 1998 and 2002. In his reelection in 2002, Pryor received the highest percentage of votes of any statewide candidate.

Judge Pryor is a graduate, magna cum laude, of the Tulane Law School. There, he was editor in chief of the *Tulane Law Review*, a member of Order of the Coif, recipient of the George Dewey Nelson Memorial Award for the graduate with the highest grade point average in the common-law curriculum, and a charter member and president of the Tulane Federalist Society.

After graduation, Judge Pryor served as a law clerk for Judge John Minor Wisdom of the U.S. Court of Appeals for the Fifth Circuit.

Following his judicial clerkship, Pryor engaged in a private practice of litigation in Birmingham and, for six years, served as an adjunct professor of admiralty at the Cumberland School of Law of Samford University. Since 2006, Judge Pryor has served each fall semester as a visiting professor of federal jurisdiction at the University of Alabama School of Law.

Judge Pryor is a member of the American Law Institute, the Board of Advisory Editors of the *Tulane Law Review*, and the Board of Advisory Editors of the *Yale Law & Policy Review*. He is a life fellow of the Alabama Law Foundation, a former vice president of the Alabama Center for Law and Civic Education, and a former chairman of the Federalism and Separation of Powers Practice Group of the Federalist Society. In 2002 and 2003, Pryor served as a member of the State and Local Senior Advisory Committee of the White House Office on Homeland Security. Judge Pryor has been awarded honorary doctorates of law from John Marshall Law School in Atlanta and Regent University in Virginia.

Judge Pryor has lectured and published widely. He has lectured at the Ronald Reagan Presidential Library and several law schools and universities. He has published in the *Columbia Law Review*, the *Virginia Law Review*, the *Harvard Journal of Law & Public Policy*, the *Yale Law & Policy Review*, the *Tulane Law Review*, the *Alabama Law Review*, the *Florida Law Review*, the *Ohio State Journal of Criminal Law*, the *Notre Dame Journal of Law, Ethics & Public Policy*, and the *Cumberland Law Review*. He has published op-eds in the *Wall Street Journal*, the *New York Times*, the *Washington Times*, and *USA Today*. He has testified before committees of the U.S. Senate on capital punishment, environmental law, and the role of the judiciary. A champion debater in college, Pryor has debated at National Lawyers Conventions of the Federalist Society, on NPR, and at the Oxford Union in the United Kingdom.

Mark L. Rienzi

Mark L. Rienzi is an associate professor at The Catholic University of America, Columbus School of Law. Professor Rienzi teaches constitutional law, religious liberty, torts, and evidence. He has been voted Teacher of the Year three times by the student bar association. His scholarship on constitutional law, religious liberty, torts, and evidence has appeared in a variety of prestigious journals, including the *Harvard Law Review*, the *Fordham Law Review*, the *Emory Law Journal*, the *Notre Dame Law Review*, and the *George Mason Law Review*. His writing has also appeared in such lay publications as the *New York Times*, the *Washington Times*, *USA Today*, *Roll Call*, *U.S. News and World Report*, the *National Review Online*, the *New York Daily News*, the *Chicago Sun-Times*, and the *National Catholic Register*. He has appeared on various television and radio outlets, including CNN, NBC, ABC, Fox News, and NPR.

As a litigator, Professor Rienzi has represented a range of parties asserting First Amendment claims in courts across the country. For 14 years, Professor Rienzi represented parties challenging the Massachusetts abortion clinic buffer zone, finally prevailing in a 9–0 decision at the Supreme Court in *McCullen v. Coakley* (2014). Professor Rienzi also successfully represented pharmacists challenging an Illinois law forcing all pharmacists to sell the week-after pill and morning-after pill, as well as pro-life pregnancy centers challenging speech regulations.

Professor Rienzi is also senior counsel at the Becket Fund for Religious Liberty, a nonprofit, nonpartisan religious liberties law firm dedicated to protecting the free expression of all religious faiths. At the Becket Fund, Professor Rienzi has represented a variety of parties at the Supreme Court, including in *Little Sisters of the Poor v. Sebelius* (emergency order, 2014); *Burwell v. Hobby Lobby* (2014); *Wheaton College v. Burwell* (emergency order, 2014); *Holt v. Hobbs* (2015); and *Zubik v. Burwell* (2016).

Previously, Professor Rienzi served as counsel in the Supreme Court and Appellate Practice Group at Wilmer Hale LLP. Before joining Wilmer Hale, he served as law clerk to the Hon. Stephen F. Williams, senior circuit judge for the U.S. Court of Appeals for the D.C. Circuit. Professor Rienzi was an editor of the *Harvard Law Review*. He earned his JD from Harvard Law School and his BA from Princeton University, both with honors.

Ilya Shapiro

Ilya Shapiro is a senior fellow in constitutional studies at the Cato Institute and editor-in-chief of the *Cato Supreme Court Review*. Before joining Cato, he was a special assistant/adviser to the Multi-National Force in Iraq on rule-of-law issues, and he practiced at Patton Boggs and Cleary Gottlieb.

Shapiro is the coauthor of *Religious Liberties for Corporations? Hobby Lobby, the Affordable Care Act, and the Constitution* (2014). He has contributed to a variety of academic, popular, and professional publications, including the *Wall Street Journal*, the *Harvard Journal of Law & Public Policy*, the *Los Angeles Times*, *USA Today*, the *Weekly Standard*, the *New York Times Online*, and the *National Review Online*. He also regularly provides commentary for various media outlets, including CNN, Fox News, ABC, CBS, NBC, Univision and Telemundo, the *Colbert Report*, and NPR.

Shapiro has testified before Congress and state legislatures and, as coordinator of Cato's amicus brief program, filed more than 200 friend-of-the-court briefs in the Supreme Court, including one that *The Green Bag* selected for its "Exemplary Legal Writing" collection. He lectures regularly on behalf of the Federalist Society, is a member of the Legal Studies Institute's board of visitors at The Fund for American Studies, was an inaugural Washington Fellow at the National Review Institute and a Lincoln Fellow at the Claremont Institute, and has been an adjunct professor at the George Washington University Law School. In 2015, the *National Law Journal* named him to its list of 40 "rising stars" in the legal community.

Before entering private practice, Shapiro clerked for Judge E. Grady Jolly of the U.S. Court of Appeals for the Fifth Circuit. He holds an AB from Princeton University, an MSc from the London School of Economics, and a JD from the University of Chicago Law School (where he became a Tony Patiño Fellow).

Jonathan Zimmerman

Jonathan Zimmerman is professor of education and history and director of the history of education program at the Steinhardt School of Culture, Education, and Human Development at New York University. He also holds an appointment in the Department of History of New York University's Graduate School of Arts and Sciences.

A former Peace Corps volunteer and high school teacher, Zimmerman is the author of *Campus Politics: What Everyone Needs to Know* (Oxford, 2016), *Too Hot to Handle: A Global History of Sex Education* (Princeton, 2015), *Small Wonder: The Little Red Schoolhouse in History and Memory* (Yale, 2009), *Innocents Abroad: American Teachers in the American Century* (Harvard, 2006), *Whose America? Culture Wars in the Public Schools* (Harvard, 2002), and *Distilling Democracy: Alcohol Education in America's Public Schools, 1880–1925* (Kansas, 1999).

His academic articles have appeared in the *Journal of American History*, the *Teachers College Record*, and the *History of Education Quarterly*. Zimmerman is also a frequent op-ed contributor to the *New York Times*, the *Washington Post*, the *New Republic*, and other popular newspapers and magazines.

Cato Institute

Founded in 1977, the Cato Institute is a public policy research foundation dedicated to broadening the parameters of policy debate to allow consideration of more options that are consistent with the principles of limited government, individual liberty, and peace. To that end, the Institute strives to achieve greater involvement of the intelligent, concerned lay public in questions of policy and the proper role of government.

The Institute is named for *Cato's Letters*, libertarian pamphlets that were widely read in the American Colonies in the early 18th century and played a major role in laying the philosophical foundation for the American Revolution.

Despite the achievement of the nation's Founders, today virtually no aspect of life is free from government encroachment. A pervasive intolerance for individual rights is shown by government's arbitrary intrusions into private economic transactions and its disregard for civil liberties. And while freedom around the globe has notably increased in the past several decades, many countries have moved in the opposite direction, and most governments still do not respect or safeguard the wide range of civil and economic liberties.

To address those issues, the Cato Institute undertakes an extensive publications program on the complete spectrum of policy issues. Books, monographs, and shorter studies are commissioned to examine the federal budget, Social Security, regulation, military spending, international trade, and myriad other issues. Major policy conferences are held throughout the year, from which papers are published thrice yearly in the *Cato Journal*. The Institute also publishes the quarterly magazine *Regulation*.

In order to maintain its independence, the Cato Institute accepts no government funding. Contributions are received from foundations, corporations, and individuals, and other revenue is generated from the sale of publications. The Institute is a nonprofit, tax-exempt, educational foundation under Section 501(c)3 of the Internal Revenue Code.

CATO INSTITUTE
1000 Massachusetts Ave., N.W.
Washington, D.C. 20001
www.cato.org